# Winning the Talent War

# Winning the Talent War

A Strategic Approach to Attracting, Developing and
Retaining the Best People

Charles Woodruffe

JOHN WILEY & SONS, LTD

Chichester • New York • Weinheim • Brisbane • Singapore • Toronto

National        01243 779777
International   (+44) 1243 779777
e-mail (for orders and customer service enquiries):
cs-books@wiley.co.uk
Visit our Home Page on http:www.wiley.co.uk
             or http:www.wiley.com

*Other Wiley Editorial Offices*

John Wiley & Sons, Inc., 605 Third Avenue,
New York, NY 10158-0012, USA

WILEY-VCH Verlag GmbH, Pappelallee 3,
D-69469 Weinheim, Germany

Jacaranda Wiley Ltd. 33 Park Road, Milton,
Queensland 4064, Australia

John Wiley & Sons (Asia) Pte Ltd, 2 Clementi Loop #02–01,
Jin Xing Distripark, Singapore 129809

John Wiley & Sons (Canada) Ltd, 22 Worcester Road,
Rexdale, Ontario M9W 1L1, Canada

*Library of Congress Cataloging-in Publication Data*
Woodruffe, Charles.
    Winning the talent war : a strategic approach to attracting, developing, and retaining
the best people / Charles Woodruffe.
        p.   cm.
    Includes bibliographical references and index.
    ISBN 0-471-98753-0 (alk. paper)
    1. Employees—Recruiting.   2. Employees—Training of.   3. Job satisfaction.
    4. Labor turnover.   I. Title.
    HF5549.5.R44W663   1999
    658.3—dc21                                                    99-31482
                                                                      CIP

*British Library Cataloguing in Publication Data*

A catalogue record for this book is available from the British Library

ISBN 0-471-98753-0

Typeset in 10/12 pt Times by York House Typographic Ltd, London
Printed and bound in Great Britain by Biddles Ltd, Guildford and King's Lynn.
This book is printed on acid-free paper responsibly manufactured from sustainable
forestation, for which at least two trees are planted for each one used

# Contents

# Acknowledgements

I had the idea to write this book about two years ago in the spring of 1997. I posted it to John Wiley a few days ago at the start of the spring of 1999. The fact that I have finished it owes a lot to other people. For a start, there is obviously the army of people whose ideas have shaped my own. This covers both the authors I have never met, as well as colleagues and clients who have been kind enough to share their thinking with me. Aside from this intellectual input and as important for this book's completion have been those people who have been invaluable to my getting it finished. Banishing interruptions has not been easy. Like London buses, for which you wait hours and then three come along at once, so it can be with consultancy. We have been consistently busy these past two years. The fact that the book is done owes everything to my colleagues, Lindsay Dagg, Julia Smith and Jo Rees, who have all worked around my part-time status the last few months, and shouldered a great deal of responsibility.

After John Wiley and I had agreed a synopsis in October 1997, I did not have a lot to show a year later and was probably heading for a five-year completion with a deadline that was already one month overdue. What galvanized me into action was a brief conversation with Linda Holbeche from Roffey Park after a talk she gave on her high-flyer research. This was followed the very next day by lunch with Claire Plimmer of John Wiley. Both made me feel it would be a shame not to focus and finish.

The subsequent six months were at times a walk along a tightrope between despair and quiet satisfaction. The fact that I stayed on the tightrope owes much to the consistent support of another colleague, Wendy Lyons. Her brand of gentle criticism ('I think I'm a little lost') mixed with praise kept me thinking the whole project was worth while even if there were chunks to be rethought and rewritten. I hasten to add that there are still plenty of examples of where I have ignored Wendy's doubts and any ideas that seem crazed or incomprehensible are no doubt the result of my being stubborn.

Then, there are people who do not even know they have helped. Most important are a band of priceless friends and particularly Linda, Jon, Ruth and George Norman. I should also like to mention Richard Churchman at my tennis club. For months he asked 'How's the book, Charles?' until I feel it struck him as ill-mannered. Mischievously, I am particularly glad to be able to demonstrate to him that he did not need to stop enquiring.

To them all, much thanks. So there we are. It is a beautiful spring day and I am glad to be able to enjoy it with no book to write. The mood will pass however! As if to illustrate the first chapter, contact is easy, courtesy of information technology. I would be delighted to hear from you, wherever you might be and my e-mail address is cw@humanassets.co.uk

# Introduction. Focusing through a fog

Flared trousers were in fashion; then they were out; now they are fashionable again. Careers in organizations were the norm; careers were dead; are careers now back in fashion? It is odd to recognize, but true, that fashion extends to management almost as much as to trousers. Where management is different is that the unfashionable does not simply disappear. It just ceases to be a priority, a focus of attention. I trust that I am not totally out of touch with the management fashions in writing a book that will suggest that today's priority for organizations is trying to offer their talented people careers.

Careers went out of fashion for a reason. They did not seem well suited to the dynamic organizations that are needed to cope with an environment of change. That, however, is to focus on but one concern of organizations. Another concern is having high-potential staff. They are a vital component of an organization's success in both the short and the long term. In the long term they will become the leadership of the organization. In the mean time, they fill key executive positions. Choosing, developing, motivating and retaining these people are critical to success. Organizations need a strategy to cover these aspects of human resourcing, while recognizing the contemporary environment. This strategy is a vital responsibility of the people leading organizations in the present day. The objective of this book is to help the present generation of leaders to engage and retain the people who are required for current and future success. They are in short supply. There is a battle for talent. It is a battle that will decide whether an organization has the people to help it win the commercial war.

The starting point for a strategy is the complexity that organizations face both in terms of their current circumstances and that predicted for the future. This complexity can perhaps best be summed up in the first of a series of paradoxes: this first paradox is that what is known is the extent of the unknown. Organizations are increasingly aware of what cannot be known and this can be disabling to forming a long-term strategy. The environment of organizations is dealt with in the first chapter.

In response to this complex environment, organizations have been pulled in two quite different directions. The first is to aim to have what might euphemistically be called a 'a flexible' relationship with staff, hoping to take people on and let them go as required. In other words, organizations have, apparently in their own best interests, rewritten the contracts they have with their staff. Certainly, the popular perception is that we have moved into an era of impermanence, and this is the direct result of the changing nature of the environment in which organizations operate. Superficially, it is ideal for organizations to be able to take people on and let them go, as needed. However, the problem is that it fights against the second aim which is to build a cadre of knowledge workers for the future, a need which also stems from the new environment. These two responses are examined in the second and third chapters.

Some organizations have attempted to square the circle of these two approaches by trying to reserve the former approach for peripheral staff and the latter approach for the core. However, in Chapter 4, I will suggest that this separation has been far from perfect. A great deal of sophistication is needed to separate the core from the rest. As a result of the popular press with headlines on the 'death of a career' and the general backdrop of delayerings and downsizings in organizations, there is a leakage of the sense of impermanence from the periphery into the core. However, this leakage is probably a minor contributor to the core's blurred identity when it is compared with the lack in many organizations of a strategy that shows commitment to their core. Without a strategy, the core are bound to be treated as strictly temporary the moment the going gets tough. Without a strategy, the core can see they are not that special.

Chapter 5 suggests what the outcomes will be if the core come to see themselves as contingent. The positive side is the removal of paternalism and the encouragement of self-responsibility. Furthermore, the best people find they can survive and thrive outside a conventional employment relationship and might have found the new arrangements to their liking. Yet, just as talented people will always find work, so organizations will always need talented people. If organizations really have released people from the concept of a career it could well be that the organizations will be bigger losers than their staff. Thus, in another paradox, firms create extra uncertainty in the way they have responded to uncertainty. By removing the old deal of security, they have enabled people to become more self-reliant and mobile. Nowadays, organizations can be less sure that people will stay on board, and they face the various costs of having created the uncertainty. Central to these costs is seeing people walk out of the door after they have been developed at great expense. All the investment in their development leaves with them, not to mention their knowledge of the organization and its customers. In addition, there is the large cost of then replacing the people who leave.

Of course, some organizations might not have made their core feel contingent or they might have found ways of retaining people while treating them as contingent. Chapter 6 examines the evidence on the state of the relationship between organizations and their core. Not surprisingly, it is equivocal, suggesting that it is imperative that each organization takes a hard look at itself. If what you see causes you to pause for thought, I suggest that is time to look once more at the strategy for the core and at what this strategy must involve if it is to be coherent and believable.

Chapter 7 sets out a strategy that is built around gaining the commitment of talented people by offering them commitment. It aims to build in the organization's need to be responsive to the environment by treating these talented people in a way that will enable them to learn continuously and respond to change, indeed to champion it.

It is, of course, important to acknowledge that such a strategy will not be right for all organizations and that there are great pressures which lead organizations to abandon strategies in favour of expediency, living from day to day. These pressures are examined in Chapter 8. Many of them seem unconvincing. While analogies can be tedious, the glare of the fog should not cause one to drive without lights. The appropriate response is to turn on the fog-lamps – lights that are more focused on a smaller point in front. In this case the focus should be on some clear and unchanging truisms:

- Organizations will always need quality staff

- Quality staff will always be in short supply

- A strategy for securing quality staff will be a strategy for an organization's success

The second part of the book looks at how to implement a strategy of gaining the commitment of talented people by offering commitment. Chapter 9 examines how large the core should be. Chapter 10 discusses the recruitment of talented people. Chapter 11 deals with the question of knowing what qualities to look for when choosing people and Chapter 12 deals with their development. Chapter 13 addresses the culture of the organization, particularly what culture will be in harmony with the strategy. Chapter 14 deals with the various needs that talented people might bring to work, particularly their need for advancement. Finally, Chapter 15 looks at the career management of talented people, suggesting that the best way forward is partnerships between the organization and its staff.

The partnership is designed to gain the ongoing services of talented people as full-time members of staff on a 'normal' contract. However, the broad approach might well apply even for organizations who have engaged in new employment relationships with talented people, perhaps

working with them more as consultants than as full-time staff. Organizations will still want to secure and retain the services of the best of these
people and that means offering more than a fee. It means being the sort of
company for which the best people will want to work. Strangely enough,
then, organizations might find themselves trying to re-create much the
same relationship with these people that would have applied had the
organizations never let them go. The difference, of course, is commitment,
but even that will have to be reoffered by organizations if they want it in
return. The outsiders will then be insiders. Part One starts by considering
how this state of affairs has come about.

# Part One

# Creating a strategy for winning talented people

# Our changing world　　　　1

## THE LATEST FASHIONS

The end of the 1990s has seen a discernible shift in the headlines. They refer increasingly to talent wars, global shortages of talent and retaining talented people as the top priority. To take the first of three examples, a *Wall Street Journal* headline in May 1998 (Lancaster, 1998) declared 'People are "hot" again at work: a full staff is new management fad'. Six months later, Richard Donkin (1998f) wrote in the *Financial Times* under the headline 'Fighting the talent war' and reported that International Business Machines (IBM) had appointed a 'vice-president of talent'. Finally, the Conference Board Europe's 1999 Human Resources Conference was held under the theme 'Winning the battle for the best people – the key to success in the global marketplace'.

This new priority shows signs of replacing the death of the career and how there is no such thing as a job for life as the fashionable focus of attention. In turn, the death of the career itself took over from a concern with succession planning and bringing in people with the potential to grow and take over the leadership of organizations. In a generation, we seem to have come around in a circle in terms of the headlined concern of organizations: harnessing people; having as flexible an arrangement as possible with them; and now trying to secure them once again.

Headlines are, of course, simplifications. Nevertheless, they carry germs of truth. Organizations do seem to be giving renewed priority to gaining and retaining talented people. However, we are not back to where we started. Although the issue might have gone around in a circle, organizations and their environment have been transformed during the cycle. Furthermore, where we are today has a very different history from where we were a generation ago. In particular, there is now the history of the 'no job for life' message, a message that, indeed, still exists alongside the 'talent war' headline.

The coexistence of the need for talent and the 'no job for life' message introduces a choice that organizations must make in terms of their treatment of people. They must decide whether their priority is to attract and retain talent or to be as nimble as they can be, taking people on and letting them go as necessary. The choice leads to two different ways of trying to win the talent war. One way is a tactic and the other is a strategy. The tactic is to try and buy talent as needed. It might be called the headhunter alternative. The strategy is a long-term commitment to attract, develop, retain and motivate talented people. To make the choice, organizations need to be clear on the changes in the environment that have taken place since people were last 'hot'. They need to consider the context in which they operate. It is a context that has both created the choice and also made it extremely hard for organizations to opt whole-heartedly for the strategy rather than the tactic.

## THE 'GOOD OLD DAYS'

It is easy to create myths, both about the present and the past. At least as a myth, a generation ago, organizations set out to identify and grow people to be their future leaders. Organizations knew this was their agenda and a worthwhile agenda at that. People within organizations, the middle classes at any rate, enjoyed a sense of security in their careers. They had jobs and felt they were on a relatively predictable conveyor belt into the future. For example, even one of the most far-sighted writers, Schein (1978), wrote with a tone that suggested a degree of stability. He described the 'matching process' between individuals and organizations, with planning as a major activity by organizations so that they would identify their human resource needs in the short and long term. He described how organizations needed to expose people to developmental experiences 'with the explicit expectation that such experiences may not pay off for five, ten, or fifteen years until those same people have reached senior positions' (p. 9). Nowadays, such time frames would seem to take one well into the unknown. The sense of stability that enabled organizations to invest on the basis of so delayed a return must seem a fond and distant memory. Even at the time of apparent stability, there were straws in the wind for the more watchful that would suggest the good old days were numbered. Schein himself discussed how the rate of change in the world was increasing. However, by far the most prophetic vision was surely provided to readers of the *Harvard Business Review* in the year 1958. They would have been able to benefit from an article by Leavitt and Whisler (1958). It described a new technology that had begun to take hold in American business, which the authors said 'does not yet have a single established name. We shall call it *information technology*' (p. 41). Leavitt and Whisler said this new technology was bound to have a far-reaching impact.

## THE INFORMATION TECHNOLOGY REVOLUTION

The foresight of Leavitt and Whisler is capped by the fact that they even predicted when the change would take hold. They entitled their article 'Management in the 1980s', and, indeed the 1980s can be seen as having been the decade of transition. By the start of the 1990s all had certainly changed and today the 'good old days' seem a distant memory. Nowadays, the certainties have, by common consent, been taken away (Herriot and Pemberton, 1995). The senses of guaranteed predictability and of knowing what would happen have been replaced by doubts and questions.

It is now a somewhat hackneyed observation that the environment in which organizations operate has clearly changed from predictability to uncertainty. While social scientists have written about turbulent environments for decades (e.g. Emery and Trist, 1965), these conditions have now arrived for all to see. In the 1990s the pace of environmental change has stepped up and its sphere of influence has become universal. The degree of uncertainty varies between organizations, but it would be hard to find one organization that has been untouched by change. Indeed, the word 'change' could, itself, be misleading as it implies a move from one point of stability to another. The real feature nowadays is that changes have become so frequent that change itself is the one thing that is constant.

The main development was, of course, as forecast by Leavitt and Whisler. The common denominator to the transformation in the environment of organizations is information technology (IT). Management gurus abound to retell the message that we live now in an information age (Hope and Hope, 1997) or the Third Wave (Toffler, 1980).

There are three effects of IT which are of particular importance to this book. First, the burgeoning of competition. Second, the power of knowledge as the source of competitive advantage. Third, the rise of the knowledge worker. They are shown in Figure 1.1.

### IT and competition

The advent of IT has by itself quite altered the world we live in and it has made life incomparably tougher for organizations. We live in an increasingly competitive and challenging world and this has been ushered in by IT. Any example is bound to seem dated by the time you read this. That only illustrates the point. At the time of writing, a good demonstration of the competitive catalyst provided by IT is that a buyer can use the Internet to post interest in a product or service. He or she can then watch suppliers take part in an 'inverse auction' to supply the item, for example, a car.

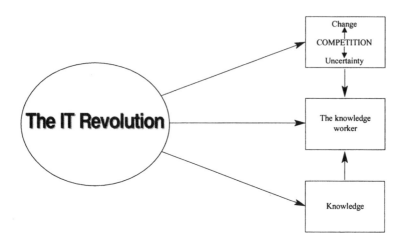

**Figure 1.1** The IT revolution and the rise of competition, knowledge and the knowledge worker

Depending on the item, the buyer can appeal to a global market of suppliers. A second demonstration of the power of IT comes from financial services. There is now a flourishing sector for remote banking. Customers are encouraged to manage their affairs via the Internet or telephone. The location of the service is unimportant. Indeed, it does not even matter whether it is provided by a bank, in the conventional sense. It can be any organization that provides banking services, not one with a building in every town dedicated solely to banking.

In swathes of the service industry, setting up and competing have never been easier. Firstly, presenting a service to the entire world can be simplicity itself. As Coulson-Thomas (1997) comments, 'within days of registration with search engines a web site may receive "hits" from visitors all over the world, and take orders direct from customers' (p. 32). Second, in many service industries, obtaining the hardware to set up is far simpler than before the advent of IT. Think of publishing and broadcasting. The equipment needed is highly accessible and 'craft' skills seem less of a prerequisite. Third, there is the ease of providing any service carried out via telecommunications. The cheapness of telecommunications makes the precise location of the organization almost irrelevant. Freephone (0800) numbers make it quite irrelevant to the customer, and the cheapness of providing such numbers makes it only marginally relevant to the organization.

An endless list of examples is unnecessary: it is quite clear that, by itself,

IT has transformed competition so that for many industries we truly live in a global market place in which competition is fast paced (Howard, 1995).

The result of these changes is that organizations have to compete harder for customers, and they have had to alter to do so successfully. Testimony to this is contained in Worrall and Cooper's (1997) survey of members of the UK's Institute of Management. These respondents described how an increasing emphasis on quality and customer care was a major driver for change. The simple truth is that, in a global market place, it is not a cliché to aspire to be world-class; for plenty of organizations it is an imperative. For many goods and services, buyers might just as well choose the world-class, rather than accepting the second best. This is particularly the case if there is no rationale to buying locally. We are also more global as consumers if the service or product being provided appears sufficiently complex or specialized to make shopping in the global market place seem worth while. These conditions apply to a wide array of products and services, including many consumer goods and, arguably, most financial services.

Many organizations must wish they had paid attention to Leavitt and Whisler (1958). The move to global competition happened quickly and it was easy to be caught unawares. For example, MacLachlan (1998a) reports how Xerox saw its dominant position in the copier market eroded to a 7 per cent share in the 1980s, having been insufficiently aware of the threat from Japan.

If the simple and direct effects of IT were not enough, IT has also promoted and then added to the effects of other simultaneous changes to the environment. These effects are outlined in Figure 1.2. In particular, the move to global competition brought about by IT is compounded by the free trade agreements which have been concluded in the 1990s. The freeing of trade shows no signs of slackening. At the 1998 'Summit of the Americas', the 34 heads of government who attended are reported (Baker, 1998) to have declared publicly their intention to establish a Free Trade Area of the Americas (FTAA) – to be completed by the year 2005 and to embrace 750 million people. These moves can readily be seen to have been triggered by IT, which has made it decreasingly possible to shelter behind trade barriers.

The waves created by IT have also ushered in a more complex range of possibilities for how organizations transact with the world. In particular, Hope and Hope (1997) note how the very way in which firms compete has become more sophisticated. They describe how 'they are now more likely to be involved in some form of economic web that will have one or two leaders (e.g., Microsoft and Intel) and a large number of followers who find niche ways to add value' (p. 8). IT and the competition it has

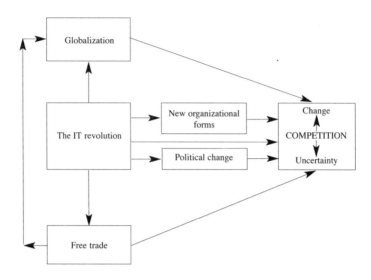

**Figure 1.2**   The direct and indirect impact of the IT revolution on organizations

encouraged can also be seen to lie behind moves towards deregulation and privatization. In order to compete in global markets, national governments enacted legislation aimed at freeing labour markets as well as deregulating industries in the late 1980s and early 1990s. These developments happened across the globe. For example, Winsborough *et al.* (1997) describe how both types of reform were enacted in New Zealand, in a manner strikingly similar to the changes in the UK. Finally, the analysis of the influence of IT can easily be extended to political changes. Most notably, access to information via satellites and the Internet is widely held to have contributed to the removal of political–economic barriers, especially the dissolution of the Soviet Union. In turn, these events have not only opened up new markets but also created potential new competition for Western companies.

These changes in the environment that can be directly or indirectly attributed to IT have, between them, transformed the uncertainty with which organizations have to deal. Essentially, the uncertainty is about the 'what', 'who' and 'how' of competition, and hence survival. What products and services are we competing against? Who is the competition? How are the competition organized? To all three questions, the answers are increasingly diverse. As examples, the 'what' for legal firms is that they compete against do-it-yourself wills; the 'who' for banks is that they compete against retail stores for customer deposit accounts; the 'how' for conventional organizations is that they compete against virtual firms with near non-existent overheads. There is no need in this book to rehearse the arguments further, except perhaps to say that the changes we have seen in two decades were unimaginable at the outset (Leavitt and Whisler, 1958, notwithstanding). It is a fair assumption that equally dramatic and unpredictable changes lie ahead. As Herriot and Anderson (1997) say, the pace of change is 'increasing exponentially, with its speed and unpredictability making long-term planning next to impossible' (p. 5). Indeed, van der Spiegel (1995) comments, 'the horizons of the new information technologies are to a large extent still unexplored' (p. 110). The growing turbulence of the environment and increasing sense of not knowing are the context in which organizations operate today.

## IT, knowledge and service

Inextricably linked to the changes brought about by IT has been another change, the rise of the power of knowledge. As Howard (1995) puts it, the move to the information age has been accompanied by a 'fundamental transformation from hand to head, capital to information, and goods to service and knowledge' (p. 23). Knowledge itself is the source of competitive advantage in more and more sectors of the economy. In line with this trend, nowadays the stock valuation of organizations is based less on physical and more on intellectual capital. Furthermore, the most rarefied valuations are offered to the firms most centrally involved in the information age, and particularly those involved with the Internet. Knowledge is the philosopher's stone of the information age.

The valuations of these firms are so high because of future prospects. Investors appear to agree with Davis (1995) when he comments that knowledge is 'an *inexhaustible* source of power' (p. 115). This property comes about because of the ability of organizations to '*learn to learn* so that their store of knowledge constantly increases over time' (p. 116).

The storing of knowledge is, itself, only possible on today's scale because of IT. Organizations can store knowledge in sophisticated databases and grant their staff access to knowledge via their intranets. They build knowledge about everything, ranging from their customers' preferences to the science and technology behind the products and services they offer. For example, Markoff (1999) reports how Microsoft had embedded within Windows 98 a system for giving each user an identification number that attached to all the documents the user created. It is reported that this feature 'has been quietly used to create a vast database of personal information about computer users'.

The power of knowledge gives an organization the power of service. The technology is available to all competitors. All firms can buy word processors, laser printers and telephone lines. They compete by what they know. What an organization knows that is unique enables it to serve its customers better than the competition.

IT, then, has made it far easier to start up in competition for a market. Perversely, it has put all competitors on a level playing field because IT carries, as Webber (1993) puts it, 'a curious paradox' (p. 26). It carries a 'self-cancelling technological advantage' (p. 26). It becomes available to anyone and ceases to offer an advantage. As a consequence, they only compete with what they know and how well they serve. In part, what they know is the 'clever stuff' of their business or profession. However, a large part of what they know is about their own customers. They 'know' their relationships. Both types of knowledge can partly be stored on the hard disks of IT. However, to be put to use, such knowledge always at some stage needs the human interface, the knowledge worker. The knowledge worker is an icon of the information age and owes an identity not just to the knowledge he or she possesses, but also to his or her attitude.

## IT and the knowledge worker

The precise definition of a knowledge worker is elusive. Handy (1991) contrasts himself with the 'sons of the toil' working the farm by his country retreat. However, where precisely does one draw the line between someone who is a knowledge worker and someone who is not? As a working definition, perhaps we can say that it is not having knowledge itself that qualifies a person as a knowledge worker. After all, taxi drivers have knowledge, but one would not think of them as knowledge workers. The knowledge worker goes a step further. He or she knows how to work with knowledge and particularly how to generate, manipulate and make useful the knowledge provided by the information age. As Figure 1.3 suggests, the knowledge worker holds the key to release the power of knowledge. Indeed, he or she *is* the key to release the power of knowledge. It requires not just intellectual skill, but also the ability, armed with the knowledge, to relate to people, particularly customers, and to solve their problems. Some knowledge workers will be better at all of this than others. They and the people who are able to lead and manage them are the talented ones in the talent wars.

The rise of the power of knowledge and the pivotal role of the knowledge worker means that the basis of competition between organizations moves to these people. They can put their firms at a competitive advantage. It is their skills, abilities and commitment that will determine the long-term success of their organizations.

As if this power was not enough, in the vast majority of organizations,

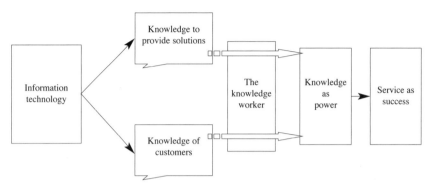

**Figure 1.3**   The key to knowledge

the knowledge workers keep some of the knowledge stored within their brains. The service organization depends upon knowledge and knowledge is diffused throughout the staff. The knowledge worker is well aware of having been given a source of power and freedom by their possession of the knowledge that is so vital to organizations. Whether or not knowledge *per se* is more important nowadays than in the past for every single job might be open to debate. What has certainly changed is the sense of independence of the knowledge worker. This independence is partly attributable to the fact that the knowledge worker owns the means of production, or can acquire them for a relatively modest sum from the local computer store.

The independence of knowledge workers is also a consequence of the deliberate moves by firms to empower them and make them free. The

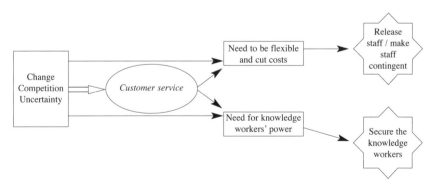

**Figure 1.4**   The customer service conundrum

empowerment and freeing of the knowledge worker have been made imperative by the manner in which many organizations have responded to the competitiveness and consequent uncertainties of the information age. They have sought to attain leanness and the ability to change rapidly.

The need to be able to change and the need for knowledge workers are, on the face of it, the recipe for a conundrum. It is presented in Figure 1.4. Answering the one need sets free the very people wanted by the second need, creating one more uncertainty for the organization to work with. Solving the conundrum is the task of a strategy for winning the talent war. The next chapter examines in more detail how organizations might have paradoxically responded to uncertainty in a way that creates further uncertainty.

# Dancing giants: the need for flexibility  2

Faced with the new environment, there can be few organizations that have not had to restructure. The main objective has been to be more flexible. At the same time, organizations have sought to reduce costs. Indeed, for many organizations, cutting costs has been an end in itself. The coupling of the need for flexibility with the imperative to control costs has entailed job losses.

The need for flexibility is ongoing. Organizations have been faced with the requirement to adapt continuously to meet the needs of customers. Mirvis and Hall (1996b) describe the new environment as one that requires firms to be free, fast and facile, to which they give the label 'the 3F organization'. Free means organizations having components that are autonomous and able to respond to changes in their own market segments. Fast means being able to respond quickly to situations and facile means being able to change thinking practices and routines.

If they have concentrated on being a 3F organization within the context of minimizing costs, organizations have been tempted to jettison the sense of their having a long-term commitment towards their members of staff. As Mirvis and Hall (1996b) put it, 'traditional career paths have become dinosaurs' (p. 74). The erstwhile commitment to people has been replaced by the notion of making them employable either inside or outside the organization.

The pressures to cut costs and to be flexible are enormous and unarguable. The problem is that answering them potentially makes it harder to be certain of securing the services of knowledge workers.

## THE NEED TO CUT COSTS

While an organization can, to an extent, accept higher costs and prices and compete on quality, it cannot simply ignore its cost base. With increased competition, this has become truer than ever. Controlled costs mean controlled prices which should mean more customers. Lower costs also potentially mean higher profits.

However, many organizations have gone well beyond controlling costs and pursued cost cutting relentlessly. It has either been the route to winning customers or a way of extracting the maximum profit from the business. Herriot and Anderson (1997) describe cost cutting as one of the strategic responses by organizations to the new competitive and uncertain environment. It has taken the form of restructuring to reduce headcount, and has involved delayering, devolution to profit centres and outsourcing of non-core activities. Hamel and Prahalad (1994) go so far as to describe the USA and UK as having produced 'an entire generation of denominator managers' (p. 9).

The scale of the reductions these denominator managers have imposed in the USA is described by Ruddle *et al.* (1998). They report that 1993 was a peak year of lay-offs in the 1990s with 600 000 people being laid off. The temptation to follow this course of action is obvious. Clay (1998) suggests that labour represents about 60 per cent of the cost of doing business. It is not surprising that organizations see employees as a 'tempting target'. So tempting, that Clay reports more than 90 per cent of medium and large organizations have laid off workers since the late 1980s. She also reminds us that the lay-offs extended to the public sector, with President Clinton having cut 172 000 workers from the federal payroll.

Ruddle *et al.* (1998) provide further illustration of just why the cost-reduction approach is so attractive. They describe how in 1996 the Fortune 500 companies grew by just 0.5 per cent in revenue, but managed to squeeze profits up by 25.1 per cent. Reichheld (1996) uses the same line of analysis. He provides a long list of US companies that have cut staff and he puts these cuts down to the fact that 'the institutional investors who drive the stock market are showing less and less patience with mediocre earnings' (p. 95). Seeming to bear this out, Berry (1999) reports how Steven M. Heller, head of mergers and acquisitions for Goldman Sachs & Co., told a conference that 'the institutional shareholder is the king of corporate governance'. He went on to say that the institution can respond to underperformance either by demanding improvement or by encouraging a hostile takeover. By way of illustration of the institutions' taste for blood, Reichheld (1996) gives the example of Xerox's stock which rose by 7 per cent on the day it announced a staff cut of 10 000. As such, Xerox conforms perfectly to Clay's (1998) report of the '7 percent rule'. The rule was coined by former US Secretary of Labor, Robert Reich, to describe the typical 7 per cent rise in a firm's stock on the announcement of downsizing.

Exactly the same pressure is exerted on organizations by investors the world over. For example, Wagstyl and Bowley (1998) report how Swantje Conrad, an analyst at J.P. Morgan, 'wants to see more action' by Siemens in terms of the degree of restructuring in which the company is engaging, despite the fact that it had inflicted heavy job losses on its staff. Relatedly, the Lex commentary column in the *Financial Times* (1998) described staff cuts at Lasmo as 'better late than never' and seemed happy to accept the cost of talented people defecting in the 'turmoil'.

The net result of the pressures in the UK has been as dramatic as in the USA. Ruddle *et al.* (1998), for example, describe the shrinkage of BP from 129 000 in 1987 to 53 000 just 10 years later. Worrall and Cooper's (1997) survey, carried out in March 1997, showed that 61 per cent of UK respondents had experienced some form of change in the 12 months prior to the survey. In just over half of these cases, redundancy had been involved. The survey also showed that 42 per cent of respondents in firms employing over 5000 people perceived their organization to be shrinking. The comparable percentage for people in firms employing under 50 people was 8 per cent, making staff reductions appear to be particularly a large organization phenomenon. Bearing out this impression, Worrall and Cooper found that the percentage of respondents in family-owned businesses (15 per cent) and private limited companies (24 per cent) who had been exposed to redundancies was much lower than for those in public limited companies (42 per cent) or the public sector (41 per cent).

A particular way of cutting the cost base has been for organizations to pursue a policy of outsourcing activities other than their core competency. For example, Cordon *et al.* (1998) report on a survey of major European corporations carried out by the Institute of Management Development (IMD) and consultants A.T. Kearney in summer 1996. It showed that just over 50 per cent expected to increase the outsourcing of their non-core activities. Cordon *et al.* attribute this to the drive to increase shareholder value and to focus on core business.

At the time of writing this book, evidence of the pressures to cut costs is as great as it has ever been. In response, there is a wave of mergers and acquisitions with the main justification being merging costs. Within the space of a few weeks in November/December 1998, Exxon and Mobil, Deutsche Bank and Bankers Trust and Zeneca and Astra all merged with the main rationale being to cut costs. The prime cost is people and all three mergers carried the promise of huge job cuts. During the same period, other organizations simply cut staff without a merger being involved. Take a typical week in December 1998. On 1 December 1998 Latour and Coleman (1998) in the *Wall Street Journal* reported that Volvo was to lay off 6000 people in an effort to reduce costs. Two days later, Parkes (1998) in the *Financial Times* described the 48 000 job losses at Boeing. Summing up the contemporary scene, Waters (1998a) reported that 'downsizing has returned with a vengeance, sweeping over companies such as AT&T and Eastman Kodak as it once swept over IBM and General Motors'. In a later article (Waters, 1998b), he describes how the first two companies are 'only now laying into mass sackings with real appetite'. Waters (1998a) describes the downsizing as the means by which organizations are trying to extract more profit from the same assets. He comments that 'only the sort of feverish, almost maniacal attention to costs and productivity demonstrated by the likes of Jack Welch, chairman of General Electric, seems capable of bringing continual success'.

## THE NEED TO BE RESPONSIVE TO CUSTOMERS

Quite apart from the need to cut costs, organizations have been delayering in order to become flexible and, so, responsive to the environment. Flexibility has meant being structured in a manner that enables organizations to respond to customers so that their needs are met rapidly. In turn, this restructuring has been associated with job losses. As Howard (1995) says, 'organizations are recruiting or downsizing employees, partly because one type of employee is being substituted for another and partly as a reflection of restructuring to become more nimble' (p. 36). In pursuing the latter objective they have delayered, reduced corporate staff and made more use of contingent workers.

Ruddle *et al.* (1998) describe how many organizations have halved to four the layers of management coming between front-line staff and the chief executive. However, this has meant lay-offs. They illustrate with the example of BP which has reduced its head office from 4000 in 1989 to 350 in 1996.

Alongside delayering, an array of writers have prescribed the end of the 'traditional' job to help organizations be nimble. For example, Bridges (1998) suggests 1990 marked the end of the 'age of the job' (p. 50) and Lawler (1994) suggests that 'the concept of an individual holding a job is no longer the best way to think about organizing and managing individuals' (p. 4). The relatively static job was ushered out by the need for greater flexibility and greater responsiveness to changing conditions. Bridges gives the example of Intel which, since the mid-1980s, has organized people in cross-functional teams working on 'assignments'. The advantage of such teams is that they can be put together specifically to respond to a particular need and composed of the people best equipped to meet that need. Mohrman and Cohen (1995) also attribute the popularity of teamworking to its being the best answer to the need to make swift responses to the environment. Although traditional jobs had stability and predictability, Mohrman and Cohen say that the hierarchical organization was simply too slow. They say that, in response, organizations have had to introduce a complex assortment of teams, such as cross-functional teams, work teams, quality improvement teams and task teams.

By itself, a move to teamwork does not threaten people's employment. It only required them to be more flexible. However, it is but a short step from putting together teams of people inside the organization to thinking in terms of bringing in outsiders to join particular teams for an assignment. Once the work is done, the team is disbanded and the outsiders cease to be the organization's responsibility.

## CONTINGENT STAFFING: THE PURSUIT OF FLEXIBILITY

The need to cut costs and the need to be nimble and responsive combine to make conventional organizations wish they could emulate the virtual organization. They have had to develop a form 'that can quickly respond to unpredictable events' (Davis, 1995, p. 120). Ideally, they would put together a team of 'associates' to fulfil the organization's current strategy and workload. Mirvis and Hall (1996b) discuss the argument that 'work will be packaged in the form of time-bounded projects and temporary assignments' (p. 78), using the term 'virtual job' to describe this way of working.

In pursuit of this ideal, people's employment has been made less secure by organizations. Cost-cutting downsizings are a clear demonstration of the loss of security. However, organizations have also been tempted to respond to the constant pressure of competition by trying to be flexible both in the promise of employment as well as in what they employ people to do. People who cease to fit have to be 'let go' because of the need to control costs. Everyone, in the modern parlance, must unrelentingly 'bring something to the party' and 'add value'.

Firms have therefore been moved to impose a contingency in their contracts with people. They behave pragmatically in the short term and have a human resource (HR) strategy that is based paradoxically on having no long-term strategy. They live flexibly, from one framing of the environment to the next. This 'just-in-time' approach is a natural reaction to living in chaos. Organizations chop and change to bring in people needed for the moment and 'trade' people to meet their immediate needs. In Herriot and Pemberton's (1995) words, under this attitude people 'may be developed and grown, but equally they may be discarded as the situation demands' (p. 11). In so doing, many organizations have veered towards treating people as if they were 'another form of economic asset' (Herriot and Pemberton, 1995, p. 11). Such contingency has various guises.

## Contingent written contracts

Contingency is written into three types of contract that have increased in popularity. First, there is the short-term contract. Cooper (1998) singles out the trend towards outsourcing and market testing as leading to the short-term contract or freelance culture, which he describes as an 'insidious work environment' (p. 75). One particular manifestation of the short-term contract is cited by Davis (1995). He discusses the trend towards virtual staff, by which he means people who are assembled temporarily to work on a particular project. They might be temporary or contract workers as well as full-time employees from one or several organizations. He says 'the preference for temporary employees reflects organizations' attempts to reduce the costs associated with maintaining permanent staff and to increase staffing and scheduling flexibility' (p. 125). However, Murray (1998) describes this as a 'worrisome' form of part-time work. She comments that 'through contingent employment, the employee works temporarily for considerably lower compensation than full-time employees'.

The second type of written contract to incorporate contingency is the part-time contract. Cooper (1998) describes how in Britain the number of men working part-time doubled in the decade to 1994 and how one in eight British workers is now self-employed. He also reports that British Telecom 'claim that more than 2.5 million people are already working wholly or partly from home' (p. 77).

The third phenomenon which fits in well with the new order is 'interim managers', who are in effect managers on short-term contracts. Donkin (1997c) reports that, although 42 per cent of employers had not even heard of the term, those that did use interim managers 'were becoming increasingly comfortable about employing them and were beginning to use them in more adventurous ways' (p. 35). Cooper (1998) also reports that the incidence of interim senior management supplied by agencies for specific projects has risen significantly.

## Contingent psychological contracts

Temporary, part-time and interim contracts make very clear to people in the written contract that their jobs are 'contingent'. Other people have received the same message in an unwritten form, via their psychological contract. Sennett (1998) quotes an AT&T executive who said, 'we have to promote the whole concept of the workforce being contingent, though most of the contingent workers are inside our walls.'

The psychological contract covers the 'unwritten understandings, values, expectations and assumptions held by the respective parties' (Kessler and Undy, 1996, p. 2). The changes to it are perhaps more fundamental than straightforward cuts in jobs. The changes to the psychological contract affect the daily lives of those who continue working in organizations.

The extent of the change to this contract is widely held to be profound. Indeed, Altman and Post (1996) starkly declare the 'social contract' between corporations and employees to be dead. In the same vein, Hall and Mirvis (1995) argue that it has been 'turned upside down in recent years' (p. 326). They contend that, in order to compete with a turbulent environment, organizations have had to promote 'career self-design' and enhance the '"learn-how" of working people' (p. 330). They describe their concept of a 'protean career', by which they mean a career that is, at will, 'shaped more by the individual than by the organization' (p. 332).

Cascio (1998) ably summarizes the new and old contract as shown in Table 2.1.

Although for some staff it has turned out to be to their liking, the alteration or cancellation of the psychological contract has been unilateral and imposed by organizations (Sims, 1994). The popular summary is that the result is generally a rather lop-sided contract. Many staff look for more than a lot of employers now offer. For example, the Conference Board (1997) carried out a survey of 92, mainly US-based, companies. They found that two-thirds 'report they once had, but no longer have, an explicit employment compact – or a tacit understanding – with their employees that promised a secure job in exchange for loyal and dedicated service' (p. 5). In the UK, Kessler and Undy (1996) talk about 'a mismatch between the employees' expectations and employers' behaviour' (p. 11).

**Table 2.1**   The old and new psychological contracts

| Old contract | New contract |
| --- | --- |
| Stability | Change |
| Predictability | Uncertainty |
| Permanence | Temporariness |
| Standard work patterns | Flexible work |
| Valuing loyalty | Valuing performance and skills |
| Paternalism | Self-reliance |
| Job security | Employment security |
| Linear career growth | Multiple careers |
| One-time learning | Lifelong learning |

Reproduced by permission of Wayne F. Cascio: On managing a virtual workplace. *The Occupational Psychologist* (1998), 35, 5–11. © The British Psychological Society.

This mismatch is, they say, a source of conflict and the Conference Board suggests the conflict is because the permanence of the change has been psychologically denied by staff.

The new psychological contract is well illustrated by one of the case studies in the Conference Board report (1997). They report that Joseph DeGennaro, VP of HR at Gemini Consulting, summarized it in the words 'Grow or go' (p. 15). He went on to explain this meant that his firm will continue to provide opportunities for employees to develop and grow, in other words providing for their employability. To remain employed, however, their contributions have to encourage the growth of the business. The same attitude is betrayed by Dauphinais and Price (1998). They describe how 'management has a new freedom to demand that workers intimately identify with their corporations and commit themselves completely to their goals. ... All workers are in a global struggle for job retention' (p. 21).

The new image conveyed by organizations is summed up by Handy (1996). He says, 'Organisations now are offering employability, not employment. That's meant to be good news but it's only organisation-speak for, "You're on your own now. Make the most of it while you're here because you won't be here very long. We can't guarantee you a job but we'll make sure that you're quite well equipped to get the next one"' (p. 35). In the same vein, Sennett (1998) says that '"No long term" might serve as the motto of modern labour'. He says his estimate is that 'a young American with at least some university training can expect to change employers at least 10 times during the course of a working life'.

Seemingly in support of Handy and Sennett, MacLachlan (1998a) quotes the Xerox resources director and HR professional as saying 'Each employee is expected to take responsibility for their own career, and for ensuring their employability, both within and outside Xerox' (p. 41).

As these quotes suggest, the key feature of the changing psychological contract is that the attitude of many organizations has altered from one of offering a commitment to one of engaging in an exchange 'for the time being'. The employment relationship is becoming shorter. People are being 'recruited, hired, and retained for their particular skills often only for the short run as organizations focus less and less on long-term performance' (Sims, 1994, p. 374). As Altman and Post (1996) put it, the employment relationship 'can stop at any time' (p. 51). It continues only while it is mutually beneficial which means that people's skills must match current business needs.

The changes to the psychological contract centre on the concept of career. Organizations seem to be conveying the message that they can no longer offer careers, let alone collaborate to manage them. Certainly, by the second half of the 1990s it appeared that many organizations had bought into the idea of 'thriving on chaos' and this extended to the whole notion of career management. Responsibility was handed over to individual members of staff, who were told to attend to their employability and build up their career portfolio. Altman and Post (1996) describe this new stance of employability as implying a minimal level of corporate responsibility for people. They place the new employment contract as somewhere between the 'immoral' and 'amoral'.

Hall and Mirvis (1995) address the implications of these changes. They say that career development will be made up more of lateral than vertical moves and people will need to develop adaptability. They also argue strongly that it is the individual who will 'own' his or her career, and suggest that 'we have to consider seriously the idea that an organization should not be in the business of career planning' (p. 335). The argument has been picked up and communicated by newspapers. For example, writing for the *Daily Telegraph*'s Appointments page, Schofield (1998) tells his readers that employers have broken the psychological contract, that 'jobs for life are endangered, if not extinct' and that 'employers now expect employees to be responsible for their own career development'.

Donkin (1995), writing at its close, saw 1995 as the year in which ' "there is no longer a job for life" must have become the most hackneyed phrase'. Even the UK education and employment secretary, David Blunkett, is reported (Donkin, 1998a) to have repeated the mantra: there can no longer be jobs for life, he said, and people leaving school might have to change *careers* up to 10 times in their working life. The report of Blunkett's speech also serves to illustrate how the message about the status of careers becomes exaggerated with the telling. Only three years earlier, the career luminaries, Hall and Mirvis (1995), had suggested that 'a person may have three or four careers in the span of his or her work life' (p. 323).

As the earlier quote from Handy illustrates, the message of 'no more jobs for life' was accompanied by another buzzword, employability. This word refers to an emphasis on making people employable both within and outside the firm. While being employable outside might remove some of the stress of potential redundancy, it must also add to people's sense of being permanently in transition between employers. Ruddle *et al.* (1998) say that 'individuals are, and have to be, far more mobile, not merely between companies but between employment and self-employment'. They therefore have to be marketable, and so organizations have directed their training at giving people marketability. It seems more than paradoxical that organizations now have to attract people by promising to equip those same people with the ability to leave. What is more, it is a paradox brought about by organizations behaving in a way that leads people to doubt how long they will be wanted.

Taking employability to its logical conclusion, Burke (1997) reports that

Rhodia, a subsidiary of Rhône-Poulenc in Brazil, has developed an employability index. The index helps 'staff predict how quickly they could find another job if they were laid off'.

The changes being described are encapsulated in the concept of the 'boundaryless career'. As described by Arthur and Rousseau (1996), these are careers that unfold across diverse employment settings. In a different jargon, there is a move from what Driver (1982) calls steady state and linear careers towards spiral (occupational switches) and transitory (frequent changes between loosely connected jobs) careers. To support their contention that boundaryless careers are becoming the norm, Arthur and Rousseau quote the statistic that the median employment tenure for US managers and professionals was just six years in 1993.

Figure 2.1 traces the main links from the need to be flexible in order that the organization can contain costs and be responsive to customers.

The move towards contingency in employment can be linked quite readily to other contemporary phenomena. Prime among these is a devaluation of age and experience in favour of youth and the possession of competencies. If organizations react to change by outplacing staff and bringing in fresh talent, that talent will tend to be relatively young. The reason is that with youth comes the perception by employers of an openness to being moulded to the organization's ways. Apparently organizations can have the best of all worlds. They can bring in people to suit their current needs in terms of competencies. They can bring them in young. What is more, these new recruits have tended to be seen as being in relatively plentiful supply. The UK has undergone a burgeoning of higher

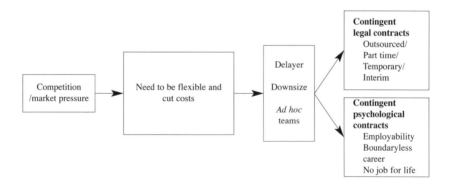

**Figure 2.1**  Making the knowledge worker contingent

education, and governments both sides of the Atlantic have kept a wedge of unemployed as a buffer against salary inflation.

The move to flexibility and 'employability' has been supported by governments in other ways. One is the advent of portable training. For example, in the UK, the National Vocational Qualifications (NVQs) and the Management Charter Initiative (MCI) both offer portability. Another is the favouring of private or personal pension schemes over company schemes. The traditional career model is perhaps best symbolized by the company pension scheme. Now we have a model whereby organizations offer employment 'for the time being' and this is symbolized by personal pension schemes.

For some writers, the boundaryless career seems to be an ideal of flexibility. For example, Saxenian (1996) deduces the virtue of open labour markets from the contrast between the Silicon Valley region and the Route 128 region of Massachusetts. The former is home of Hewlett-Packard (H-P); the latter of DEC. Silicon Valley is characterized by open labour markets and collaborative practices. H-P accepts that people leave and the company maintains congenial relations with such people, and accepts a blurring of boundaries between firms. Saxenian goes on, 'DEC, by contrast, detached itself almost completely from the region' (p. 34). She attributes H-P's comparative success and the success of the Silicon Valley region to its boundaryless attitude. DeFillippi and Arthur (1996) describe a similar type of boundaryless condition as applying to the major public accounting firms. These authors describe how young accountants gain experience and exposure to a range of clients before leaving to work for one of the clients. They then become another insider and point of contact for their erstwhile employer, the accounting firm.

Without doubt, boundarylessness has benefits. Without doubt too, the need to cut costs and the need to be flexible are clear products of the new environment. They are unarguable. It is also unarguable that staff must respond by being flexible and adaptable and taking responsibility for themselves. The old paternalism is gone. As Kahn (1996) describes it, this paternalism bred dependence, or, in some cases, a resentful counter-dependence. At its best the move away from paternalism has encouraged people to be self-reliant and to face the reality that 'no one is owed a living'. So far, so positive. However, many organizations have gone further than the acknowledgement of these simple truths. They have conveyed the attitude that employment is strictly 'contingent', by which they have meant that they feel little commitment to staff. As Kahn puts it, people feel abandonment. Not all organizations have taken the path to contingency fully; nor does it meet with universal acclaim. Nevertheless, there is a clear pressure on organizations to make people contingent, a pressure to which many have succumbed.

These changes have not been greeted passively by staff. Rousseau and Wade-Benzoni (1995) discuss the phenomenon of people suffering shifts from core to peripheral status, which, not surprisingly, is seen as a contract violation and loses their trust. In turn, this causes people to change their schemata for viewing careers. Rousseau and Wade-Benzoni say 'often the most loyal are the most affected' (p. 317) and they comment how this 'broken psychological contract can give rise to loyalty to one's own career in place of the organization' (p. 317). The result is that people see themselves as free agents using different jobs and organizations as stepping stones in their self-managed careers. As Herriot and Pemberton (1995) put it, 'the new deal isn't *relational* any more. There's no taking on trust, no mutual commitment. The new deal is a strictly *transactional* one; you give me this and I'll give you that' (p. 20). On the face of it, this does not seem the ideal relationship to have with the lifeblood of organizations, the knowledge workers.

# What about the     **3**
# knowledge workers?

If being lean and nimble is one need to have emerged from the new environment, having the resource of knowledge workers is another. The most powerful expression of the need for people as a resource is when they are part of the business strategy. Almost by definition, under those circumstances they are a resource that an organization will wish to retain, at least for as long as they remain part of the strategy. They will form a major part of the basis for the organization's value.

## THE HR STRATEGY IS THE BUSINESS STRATEGY

The HR strategy becomes the business strategy when knowledge workers are put forward as the winning resource for an organization. Seeing the people of the organization as a strategic resource for achieving competitive advantage is listed by Hendry and Pettigrew (1995) as one of the elements of the strategic theme of human resource management (HRM). The argument is that having a superior human resource means having a winning resource. It has an obvious logic. It starts from the, seemingly unarguable, premise that competitive advantage will increasingly be based upon people. It may be a cliché, but it is also true that constant change and increased competitiveness have resulted in people being the only way that firms can get an edge on one another. In particular, organizations that possess talent will have the basis for winning over their rivals. People become the strategy for success.

Bartlett and Ghoshal (1995) are strong advocates of this view. They describe the effect of the contemporary environment as being to 'shift the focus of many firms from allocating capital to managing knowledge and learning as the key strategic task' (p. 18). They describe the ability to attract and retain the best people as 'a key source of competitive advantage' (p. 18). Ghoshal and Bartlett (1998) sum up the argument saying, 'in a knowledge-based era, the scarce strategic resource that will allow one company to surpass its competitors is the quality of the people working for it'. Much the same argument is put forward by Pfeffer (1994). He describes how people are 'becoming more important because many other sources of competitive success are less powerful than they once were' (p. 6). The combination of delayering and downsizing has added a further twist to the argument, with those who remain in the organization becoming more important than ever (Meyer and Allen, 1997).

There is then a powerful line of thinking that sees people as critical to success. It is moreover an argument that is being accepted by organizations. As Lado and Wilson (1994) observe, 'some of the most admired American corporations have placed human resource issues at the center of their strategic mission and vision' (p. 709).

One manifestation of this line of thinking lies in the concept of organizational competencies. These specify what the organization is particularly good at. For example, Hewlett-Packard are particularly good at making printers, and Nokia have built a similar reputation with mobile telephones. Sony are particularly good at making portable music equipment, the Walkman having becoming a household name. Many years before, Hoover built the same type of reputation for its vacuum cleaners. Organizational competencies, then, are the products and services that set the firm apart from its competitors. The organizational competency approach is championed by Hamel and Prahalad (1994). They advocate a business strategy based around core competence leadership. The organization needs, as best it can, to discern future opportunities and build the core competencies to exploit those opportunities. It needs to do so in the context of change and chaos. Building core competencies means building them in people as well as equipment. They are ultimately skills that reside in staff and so people are the basis of the business strategy.

## TALENT AS A RESOURCE THAT NEEDS TO BE RETAINED

If people are the basis of the business strategy then their retention must be as paramount as their recruitment. As Foster (1998) comments, 'the real tragedy is that organisations often do not realise the value of what is walking out of the door until it is too late' (p. 11). There is, indeed, a series of reasons for the importance of retention, starting with retaining the competencies that set the organization apart from its competitors.

## Retaining knowledge of competencies

Organizational competencies take time to build. It requires commitment and transcends products and business units. Clearly it is vital to the organization that it can retain the people in whom the competencies reside. It is also vital to retain the people who are committed to building the competencies, the people who are their champions. Indeed Hamel and Prahalad describe as 'key' the stability of senior management teams because they offer stability to the strategic agendas.

Retention is, therefore, implicit in a business strategy based around people as the winning resource. If people are not retained, the organization loses the knowledge of its competencies. Pfeffer (1994) discusses how people need to be treated as permanent rather than contingent members of the organization if the organization is to hope to capture the benefits of any firm-specific knowledge or capabilities that they may develop. What is more, if people leave, not only are competencies lost *from* the organization, they are lost *to* another organization.

## Retaining a scarce resource

Williams and Dobson (1997) argue that the criticality of people is increased in a turbulent environment. They go on to suggest that, in this sort of environment, the organization will select people for their potential for training and retraining rather than focusing on the behaviours they are capable of at a particular time. These behaviours will become obsolete, but the ability to acquire new behaviours will be an enduring asset. In essence, the argument is that 'talent' includes 'trainability' and 'retrainability' and that this is a scarce commodity. Only a small proportion of people might be able to acquire and deliver the organization's unfolding competencies. Once found they need to be retained.

Donkin (1998c) reports that the phenomenon of a talent shortage has become a 'sexy subject'. It is now being labelled a 'global executive talent famine' by the headline writers. Donkin reports a survey of 150 large international companies. It asked about the greatest obstacles to growth until 2002. More than one-third of the companies replied in terms of finding and retaining talent as well there being a lack of management capabilities. Hunt (1999a) describes the major function of the HR professional as being 'to ensure the supply of talent necessary for the company to achieve its objectives'. He also observes that it is the line manager's responsibility to oversee the supply and development of talent.

The business case for retaining people is illustrated by Griffith (1998a) who reports how Steve Jobs the CEO of Apple argues that a good person is worth 50 mediocre workers. A particularly dramatic illustration of the scarcity and value of talent was provided by Timmins (1998). He describes how a single unfilled job at Sun Microsystems was thought to cost the company $700 000–$800 000 a year. The rationale was that, without a post-holder, the company is unable to make progress in reducing cost overruns. At the time, there were apparently 2300 unfilled positions at Sun, 1200 of which were in core IT posts.

## Retaining customers

Aside from the organizational competencies, another specific form of knowledge that is vital to organizations concerns customers. The organization's knowledge of its customers, and the customers' knowledge of the organization is through the staff. As Reichheld (1996) observes, these relationships with customers take time to build. It follows that losing staff means the potential loss of customers.

A vivid illustration is provided by the music industry. As Welch (1998a) reports, Polygram's '16 500 employees are seen as crucial to retaining the major artists who comprise the industry's "assets"'. These artists are more bound to the people who handle them than to the label. This has led Polygram to try to tie its staff in with financial incentives, worried that they might leave as a result of the merger with Seagram. As a second example, Stewart (1997) describes the loss of Maurice Saatchi from the advertising agency, Cordiant. He took with him other directors as well as key clients including British Airways and Mars. The share price halved.

The same is true to a greater or lesser degree for any 'relationship' business. Losing a member of staff potentially loses the relationship with the customer. While organizations can take steps to retain the customer relationship when the member of staff leaves, the far easier path is to retain the member of staff.

## Retaining an expensive investment

Graduates in the UK are said to cost an average of over £4500 each to recruit and to have £60 000 spent on them in order to produce a return. Huselid (1995) specifies reaping the returns from the investment of training people as one of the benefits of a strategy to retain people. Reichheld (1996) presents an economic model developed by the consulting firm Bain. This shows seven economic effects associated with employees' loyalty. The figure is reproduced in Figure 3.1. The figure suggests that most of the benefits start to apply after a year's employment and grow in magnitude. Indeed, Conger (1998) goes so far as to suggest that today's high potentials might need two decades before the investment in them yields 'significant returns'.

Reichheld (1996) sees the benefits as coming from the cost of recruiting people, and of training them, as well as the efficiencies gained from experience. In addition long-standing staff are better at selecting and retaining customers and they are a source of customer referral as well as employee referral.

## Retaining the tacit knowledge worker

Job success depends on tacit knowledge (Sternberg, 1997) and this is a knowledge that takes time to build up. By tacit knowledge, Sternberg

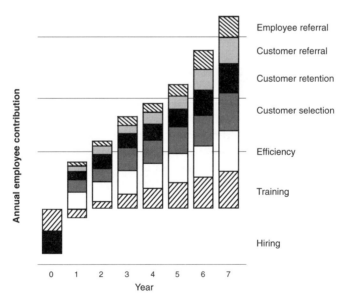

**Figure 3.1**  Why long-term employees create value. Reprinted by permission of Harvard Business School Press. From *The loyalty effect: The hidden force behind growth, profits and lasting value*, by Frederick Reichheld. Boston, MA 1996 Figure 4.1.

means the 'knowledge typically acquired on the job or in the situation where it is actually used' (p. 202). He describes it as the practical knowledge a person builds up in an organization, covering what to do when, as well as 'when and where to do it, and when and where not to' (p. 205). As such, tacit knowledge is infused with the organization's values. Measures of such knowledge typically correlate in the range 0.3–0.4 with performance, and it can therefore be considered an important influence on performance. Anderson and Ostroff (1997) describe the socialization process whereby new employees are integrated into an organization. The new people have to acquire the knowledge needed to perform their job functions. They also have to assimilate the organization's culture and climate to an extent that enables them to fit with established work practices and norms. They describe how the information covers the task (i.e. specific job demands), role (i.e. wider aspects such as networks and communication channels), group (i.e. norms and climate) and organization (i.e. values, history, goals). The result is social learning, whereby the individual's behaviour, attitude and norms are modified to achieve an enhanced person–organization fit. All this takes time, though, as Anderson and Ostroff point out, little research has been carried out on how long the timescale is. Nevertheless, quite clearly it is an investment which is lost if the person leaves and it then has to be repeated for the newcomer.

## Retaining organizational stability

Rousseau and Wade-Benzoni (1995) suggest that 'retention in the core promotes organizational stability as well as continuity and learning' (p. 308). Conversely, a rapid turnover of staff lends an air of chaos to an organization. Customers lose their points of contact, as do those in the supply chain. People within the organization continually find gaps in their networks. Turnover can beget further turnover as the norm among staff swings towards leaving.

## Retaining the future leadership

Organizations do not only need to retain people for the immediate reasons of keeping their knowledge of competencies and customers and retaining their general management talent. Retention also concerns the need to have a future leadership. If the organization believes it has the long-term future which its shareholders are presuming, then it needs to take steps to plan ahead for its long-term leadership. Part of the plan must be a strategy to retain the future leaders. Otherwise, the organization will arrive at the future with its leadership lacking in number or ill-prepared to take on their role. If the future leaders are not retained, not only does the organization lose its investment in their development. It might also not be possible to insert people of high quality into the organization when they are needed. Just such a problem is reported to be facing major UK corporations. Urry (1999) reports 'a worrying lack of talent at the pinnacle of British industry', leading the companies to struggle to replace departing chief executive officers (CEOs). While part of the reason is that people have been ill-prepared for the demands of the CEO position, another aspect is said to be that many good managers leave to run buy-outs where they can earn more money and be outside the public arena.

## A RESOURCE THAT WILL INNOVATE

Organizations want more from their knowledge workers than their presence and their retention. They want them to innovate, and in order for this to happen, people have to feel safe to take a risk. Innovation involves taking a chance and people have to trust the organization not to punish a chance that does not pay off. As Hope and Hope (1997) say, in the third wave, ideas must be harnessed and nurtured and 'this requires a new relationship between managers and workers, one based more on trust and partnership than on control and compliance' (p. 15). Only with an atmosphere of trust and mutual support will organizations foster a culture in which difficult questions can be asked about the future. Likewise Bartlett and Ghoshal emphasize trust in the establishment of a behavioural context for risk-taking.

Herriot and Anderson (1997) also stress that organizations nowadays need staff to be innovative and creative. For this to happen, people need 'a degree of security so that risks may be taken; autonomy from over-zealous control; a sense of agency such that individuals believe that they can have an impact on outcomes: and working in teams so as to benefit from diverse perspectives' (p. 7).

Innovation can be seen as the particular output of the talented person that marks him or her out from others. It also goes under the name of flair. Organizations need people to produce novel responses from the knowledge they are working with. Innovation enables the organization to steal a march on the competition. However, it is clear that having talented people is a necessary but not sufficient condition for innovation. To produce the ideas, people have to be in the right environment.

## TALENT AS THE BASIS OF THE ORGANIZATION'S VALUE

If people are as critical as the above arguments suggest, it should be the case that talent and knowledge are the basis of the organization's stock value. This is, indeed, so. Hope and Hope (1997) report that the intangible assets of manufacturing companies are now worth twice the tangible assets. For service companies, the multiple is 5 to 15 times. In line with this, the high value of human capital has been used as an explanation for the record-breaking stock prices on the Dow and FTSE (Taylor, 1997). Prices seem high in terms of the old yardstick, Tobin's Q. This divides the stock market value of assets by their book value. However, prices may be less stretched than Tobin's Q suggests because it does not take account of the level of intellectual capital held by companies.

High stock values are based on a high and growing earnings stream that capital provides. In the short term earnings can be boosted by cutting costs; in the long term they are boosted by adding value to the capital. In the information age, the added value comes from people. Self-evidently, the stock price of high-technology companies would not be sustained if the intellectual assets were in jeopardy. According to one scenario, then investors will be increasingly aware of the strategies for building and retaining high-potential staff when making their investments. Essentially, the investment is in those staff. The organizations with the better strategies will be more successful.

An example of one such investor is provided in Michael's (1998) description of a fund manager, Anthony Cross. Cross runs River and Mercantile's first Smaller Companies Fund. Cross is said to favour companies with intellectual capital as well as employee share ownership. He talks about choosing companies with the 'people-related strengths, which motivate and retain their key employees' (p. 10) One of his top tips is 'if you feel that a company's intellectual capital is weakening, sell the shares'. (p. 11).

Reichheld (1996) reports that over a three-year period the stock of S&P 500 companies that downsized lagged others by 24 per cent. This might suggest other investors agree with Cross. Reichheld comments, 'This really should come as no surprise. Companies forced to jettison their human assets *should* be worth less' (p. 95). Conversely, Clay (1998) draws attention from the same survey (carried out by Cascio and his colleagues at Colorado's Graduate School of Business) that 'the companies that did the best had actually *upsized*'. Clearly it is just as possible that firms in the survey upsized because they were doing well as that they did well because they upsized. Nevertheless, the result at least suggests a relationship between intellectual capital and stock values.

Anthony Cross's approach would presumably meet with the endorsement of David Ulrich. He is reported by MacLachlan (1998b) as predicting to the 1998 Society for Human Resource Management (SHRM) annual conference that 'Within five years, a top HR person will change his or her firm, and the stock price will change too' (p. 36). Presumably, the logic is that with this person will go the key to building and retaining the organization's intellectual capital.

Not all investors take the detailed interest in HR strategy shown by Anthony Cross or forecast by Ulrich. Indeed, perhaps few do. Nevertheless, they are interested in the result of the strategy, namely the long-term future of the organization. However, professional investors have also been characterized as having a short-term view, and this was discussed in Chapter 2. They have insisted on cuts to boost profits.

## THE FUNDAMENTAL PARADOX

This points up very clearly the paradoxical world that confronts organizations. Nobody buys a company that does not appear to have a long-term future. While investors can move at the click of a mouse, they move to stocks with the best long-term future. The short-term view focuses on the long term and not on cost cutting. The stream of future profits and payments is the essential basis of the stock value.

However, as Figure 3.2 illustrates, investors also want to maximize this year's profits. They are constant potential sellers on short-term considerations. This twin pressure of the long and short term is communicated to the organization's management creating the oscillation between the need to build the intellectual capital of the organization and the need to be flexible and keep down costs. The short term is by its very nature the more insistent. It courts the danger that steps taken for the short term will compromise the long term. Equally, the long term is of little use without a short term.

We arrive then at the central paradox that organizations face. People are clearly important. They are the knowledge workers. They are the customer interface. They are the talent. However, the twin truth is that they are also a cost. They might also go past their 'sell by' date. The issue that confronts organizations is how to reconcile the need to build a resource with the need to be flexible and minimize costs.

Treating people as a resource has the sense of being a long-term approach. It is the very long-term nature of some of the arguments that is their weakness. CEOs and boards are measured by this quarter's figures by investors who can sell their stock if the going gets tough. The dilemma is ably summarized by Hope and Hope (1997) who ask, 'Do managers see their primary role as meeting the short-term demands of shareholders or ensuring the long-term survival of the company?' (p. 43).

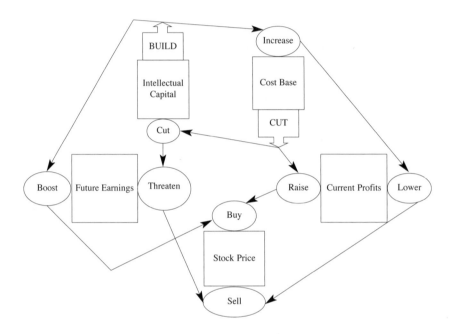

**Figure 3.2**  The investor's conundrum

# Squaring the circle    4

The paradox of the conflict between the short and the long term is not new. However, it is thrown into sharp focus by the new competitive environment. This environment has emphasized the constant presence of the two needs. First, the need to build and retain a resource of talented people. Second, the need to be flexible and minimize costs. Each leads to a distinct attitude towards people. People are a resource to be nurtured, or people are a cost to be incurred as flexibly as possible.

The two needs and attitudes are related to two different types of psychological contract that the organization might have with people. Rousseau (1990) uses the terminology of 'relational' and 'transactional' to describe these contracts. The former is concerned with the ongoing relationship between the organization and the person and seems suited to answering the need for people as a resource. The transactional contract refers to specific exchanges of money for the provision of skill and seems appropriate if people are a cost.

Like the two needs, the attitudes and contracts have existed side by side for at least this century. The period of scientific management saw an ascendancy of people being treated as a cost with transactional contracts. They were labour in industry and cannon fodder in war. Then the human relations period that took hold of management thinking after World War II gave greater priority to people as a resource with relational contracts. They were to be treated to the more sensitive approach of the manager who sees people as intrinsically motivated, and needing the right conditions for them to contribute to organizational objectives. The manager who sees people in this way was labelled as having a Theory Y approach by McGregor (1960), in contrast to the Theory X approach that sees people as a cost needing command and control and galvanized into action by money.

The scientific manager might have acknowledged the resource people provide and the Theory Y manager might have acknowledged the cost they incur. However, it seems fair to say that the attitude of seeing people as a cost dominated the former manager's view, while seeing people as a resource dominated the latter's. The nature of people's motivation imputed by Theory X and Theory Y might have altered by the turn of the millennium, but the basic attitudes of people being a cost or resource remains. What is different about the current period is that the two attitudes seem almost equal in their insistence. People are a resource. People are a cost.

Each line of thinking has its own logic and, taken on its own, seems to lead to a desirable course of action. If the need for people as a resource were taken alone, the obvious way forward would be for organizations to fight the talent war with a long-term strategy to grow and retain people. The organization would aim for a relationship with people. On the other hand, if only the need for organizational flexibility is considered then treating people as contingent seems entirely appropriate. The organization would have a transaction. One focus aims for an organization of committed staff who are to be retained. The other appears to conclude with a virtual organization of the fourth wave (Miles and Snow, 1996). It is made up of professional knowledge workers who have 'shore lines' to several other virtual organizations concurrently.

The problem is that making progress with either choice is likely to be constrained by the other need reasserting itself. Consider the first choice which focuses on people as a resource. The organization would head down the path of having a relationship. Many organizations acknowledge that we are living in a time when the cliché of people being the most important asset has never been more apposite. Assets need to be retained and treated as capital. These organizations see fully that the acquisition, development and retention of people are vital to their competitiveness in the market place and to their esteem on the stock exchange. In these circumstances a relationship seems more appropriate and certain than a transaction as a way to husband the resource. However, they are faced with a permanent temptation to have the relationship on their own terms, in particular, for as long as it suits them. In other words, the need for flexibility is likely to reassert itself and the temptation is to oscillate back to having a transaction. Succumbing to this means jettisoning the long-term strategic response in favour of the short-term need to keep profits growing each quarter.

Alternatively, consider an organization which has decided to meet its need to be able to change by engaging in transactions. Almost by definition, a transaction means no lasting commitment. People would be best advised to leave if a better transaction is on offer elsewhere. Yet, if they are to thrive in the environment that has made knowledge the key, organizations need the long-term commitment of staff. Indeed, as we saw in Chapter 3, having a stability among staff has been put forward by Pfeffer (1994) and Reichheld (1996) as a strategy for competitive advantage. Organizational competencies reside in staff and so staff need to be retained. The approach that emphasizes transactions carries the price that people might not still be around as a resource when they are needed. They might have moved on to a more rewarding transaction, perhaps one that promises a relationship. The pure transaction carries with it no logical basis for staying a moment longer than it offers the best available deal to the talented person. Organizations that have made people mobile are finding they now have to cope with a talent war.

Of course, some organizations might concentrate on just one of the needs, apparently unperturbed by the other. For example, some organizations might not treat their staff as the prized source of competitive advantage. Either they do not feel the need for a resource, or the desire to control costs and maintain flexibility is far more persuasive than the desire to build and retain a resource. They run the risk of destroying organizational competencies or, at least, preventing the full exploitation of those competencies (Lado and Wilson, 1994). Such firms should be at a competitive disadvantage against those who have built and retain a winning resource. Equally, some organizations may not perceive the need to be responsive to customers and able to change. They run the risk of a rude awakening.

Notwithstanding such failures to perceive it to be the case, the two needs are the reality for virtually all organizations and the vast majority of them are focused on both of the needs to a greater or lesser extent. They will seek to satisfy both needs at the same time or at least to satisfy one while not jettisoning the other. Broadly, organizations have taken two approaches to this squaring of the circle. One is to try to have it both ways with the same people, giving them both the message that they are a resource and the message that they are a cost. The other approach is to give different messages to different people, hoping to satisfy the need for a resource with some people and the need for flexibility with others.

## HAVE IT BOTH WAYS: JUST ANOTHER ASPECT OF OUR POSTMODERN AGE

There are many organizations that communicate to people that they are a resource but that they are also a cost. For example, as Pfeffer (1998) observes, organizations tend to say one thing (you are our greatest asset), but do another (lay off experienced employees). They seem to be opting to leave it to staff to make their own sense of a complicated world. These organizations might be persuaded by the equal weight of the two approaches and see them as existing alongside one another. As described by Pucik (1998), they try to maximize both sides of the contradiction. The notion that contrary threads can be true at the same time is in keeping with the postmodern (Jencks, 1996) era in which we live, and needs to be examined as part of that contemporary movement. Currently, we are asked to accept contradictions and paradoxes just because it is the post-modern thing to do. It is as if contradiction had suddenly become acceptable, indeed rather chique. The postmodern condition is described by Jencks as one in which there is a duality or Janus face to events, summed up by the question, 'do you want the good news or the bad news first?'. For example, the good news is we are going to make you employ-able; the bad news is you might not be employed in this organization. The postmodern era is a time of pluralism in which competing ideas and fashions exist together because change happens so rapidly that 'all fash-ions are in fashion' (p. 58). This has led to a shift in mood under which people have 'a developed taste for juxtaposition, incongruity and paradox' (p. 60).

This postmodern taste can be seen in the current literature on careers. There is the presentation of opposing 'truths'. Staff are valued but employ-ment is transitory. There is the bitter-sweet consequence for individuals of competition. What they gain as consumers they stand to lose as employ-ees. For organizations, there is a cloud for the silver lining of flexibility: they create for themselves the uncertainty of whether staff will stay or go.

Embedding the debate on careers within postmodernism is helpful in so far as it shows that careers are not an isolated subject matter. The state of careers is part of the wider contemporary postmodern scene. It is a scene that Jencks sees as having been created by the rise of the information society. Perversely information creates chaos rather than order. The impact of IT on organizations described in Chapter 1 is but one instance of the impact of IT on our whole world. The result is the turbulence of postmodernism.

Some aspects of postmodernism can be positive and liberating. In architecture, it has taken us away from the constraints of modernist tower blocks. In the context of management, it can be seen as offering the opportunity of freeing organizations of the restrictions of trying to be uniform with each other in their approach. Kay (1998), for example, argues that we now need postmodern management just as we previously needed postmodern architecture. He suggests that management is stuck in a modernist phase whereby the attempt is made to structure all organiza-tions on the same lines. A postmodern diversity of approach between organizations would be welcomed. However, postmodernism seems less appropriate when it takes the form of contradictions by a single organiza-tion in terms of its treatment of people's careers. It does not seem satisfactory simply to say that the existence of opposites is part of the postmodern condition and we had better learn to live with it. The limitation is that people tend to look for one overriding message in the different messages they are given. People welcome simple truths. This presumably is the whole basis of statements of visions and values espoused by today's organizations. It is also, perhaps, the basis of Hunt and Laing's (1997) finding that more competent business leaders 'espouse quite clear values which they repeat and repeat' (p. 40).

While those who are more tolerant of ambiguity or preferring complexity might be more tolerant of contradiction, one message is likely to be more powerful than the other. If organizations say you are part of our succession plan, yet your post is insecure, the truth is you are insecure.

As Bayliss (1998) aptly puts it, 'it will not do to rely on the rhetoric that "people are our most important asset" if the reality is quite different' (p. 14). The message of contingency prevails over any message of being the greatest asset.

There is indeed an intellectual laziness in trying to offer conflicting messages to the same people and to explain it away as part of the postmodern condition. One could go further and say that some organizations are being downright cynical in what they are trying to achieve. They attempt to sweet-talk people with the suggestion that they are a resource, while all the time seeing them as strictly time-limited. For example, McGuire (1998) describes how 'psychologists and organizations' are collaborating so organizations will 'be able to regularly recruit and hang on to good employees who will be committed to a job even though it may not be committed to them' (p. 10).

Whether motivated by laziness or cynicism on the organization's part, the result is the same. Once they see the simultaneous and contradictory messages, people will draw the conclusion that they are contingent. The organization then has to try to retain people and win the talent war by the tactic of a transaction. The aim is not to build a resource but to hang on to people for as long as they are needed. That is precisely the message of contingency. The transaction approach is an 'off-the-shelf' approach. The organization buys people when they are needed and tries to retain them for as long as they are needed by giving them what they want in the 'here and now'. The problem is that they might not obediently swallow the bait for as long as it is on offer.

## CREATE A SHAMROCK

One way around the problem of conflicting messages is to give the different messages to different groups. This way forward is suggested by Clarke (1998). He says, 'while it can be argued that all employees are knowledge workers to some extent, some *are* more important than others'

(p. 48). The more important become a resource; the less important a cost. The more important are the core; the less important the periphery. Within this spirit, Mirvis and Hall (1996a) analyse the overall change in the psychological contract as a shift from relational to transactional, but temper this with the hypothesis that core staff will be more likely to have a relational contract.

One of the best-known exponents of making distinctions between staff is Handy (1991). He uses the analogy of the shamrock, with the first leaf representing the core. They are the full-time permanent employees. The second leaf is the contract staff and the third is the workforce of part-time and temporary staff. Handy sees this parallel existence as the way forward. In Handy's clover leaf organization, the core is treated more as a resource while the periphery is treated more as a flexible cost.

Others divide the core and the periphery slightly differently from Handy. Jackson (1997) describes how the core can be seen as the *inner* group of permanent staff. The peripheral workforce is divided into, first, those who are full-time employees but with less job security and less access to career opportunities, and, second, people who are on non-standard contracts, such as part-time staff and temporary staff. A survey in 1993, reports Jackson (1997), showed 38 per cent of people in UK employment (9.6 million people) were in the second of these peripheral workforce groups. Whatever the detailed differences, all the definitions of the core agree that they are special. Rousseau and Wade-Benzoni (1995) describe core employees as 'those round whom the organization is built' (p. 307), and they acknowledge the 'mutual attachment of core employees and organization' (p. 308). The understanding between the core and the firm is summarized by Hunt (1998b) who uses Handy's model of the organization to describe how

> contributors to the strategic core are usually involved in long-term relationships to maximize competitive advantage. Roles can be negotiated and refined over time. Some protection from the hassle of the immediate market allows these contributors to build mutual trust and develop teamwork. Suitable performance measures are established to help people learn from their experience. Subtle judgments can be made about these contributors' motivations, potential and loyalty.

Many organizations might overtly or intuitively make a distinction between the core and periphery. However, there is a danger of the segregation failing at the points of transmission and of receipt. If this happens, the core are no longer simply a resource who enjoy a relational

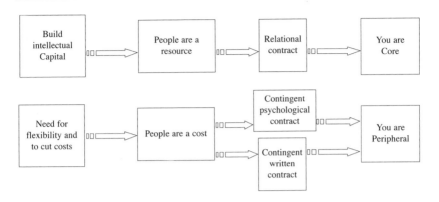

**Figure 4.1**   Mixed messages to the core

contract. They also become a cost with whom the contract is transactional. Commitment is tempered by contingency. The position is represented in Figure 4.1.

## Mixed messages: a flexible core

The need for organizational flexibility and to control costs is ever-present and waiting to reassert itself. The risk is that the message transmitted to the core runs along the lines: 'while you are a resource, you are also a cost'. The core is offered, in career terms, a variation on the same theme as the periphery. Certainly, Hall and Mirvis (1995) describe how, in future, lifetime job security will not be possible to guarantee. While this is true, literally, what is at issue is the attitude the employer adopts in making such statements. Certainly the core will not be offered a reassuring message if Hall and Mirvis's (1995) subsequent prediction is followed. It is that employers might 'offer to "trade" employees, or even whole groups, on a temporary or permanent basis as job opportunities ebb and flow between companies' (p. 343). Organizations might be tempted into this action because they always faced the need for flexibility within a context of minimizing costs. Organizations head down the path of thinking of people as a resource. Immediately, the need for flexibility reasserts itself together with the fact that even the core are a cost as well as a resource. As a result, organizations are moved back to the position of trying to have the best of both worlds. They start by treating the core and periphery separately but find themselves treating the core in some respects as if it was peripheral.

Organizations combine the relationship with their right to treat people as a cost to be incurred flexibly.

This mixed message is contained in the psychological contract for the core. Although the core might be on permanent contracts, they are different psychological contracts than in the past and, in particular, they are different from the contracts that a resource might expect. The contemporary contract for the core is described by Jackson (1997) as one by which they receive investment in their skill and gain job security by accepting functional flexibility. This involves in the short term being prepared to be flexible about their roles and in the long term it involves them accepting the need to change careers and retrain. At a basic level, this contract is simply common-sense reality. However, when it is imposed upon them with a 'take it or leave it' attitude the core will feel treated more as a cost that is begrudged than a resource. Yet, this is just the imposition which many organizations are deciding to make and the attitude they are managing to convey.

The blurring of the distinction between the core and periphery is illustrated by Rousseau and Wade-Benzoni (1995). They describe how 'organizations are currently reexamining their reliance on core employees in light of the overhead burden they bring and in the face of escalating demands for change and innovation' (p. 308). They describe the mix of employment relations that organizations increasingly use, and say this 'raises issues about the effects that the presence of both core and peripheral workers in the same organization have on each other' (p. 314). The same point is made by Howard (1995) who adds that 'not even core employees can count on long-term careers within one organization' (p. 37). In similar vein, Davis (1995) notes how the response by organizations to the need to be more flexible has been to remove internal barriers including the barrier between permanent and temporary employees.

Certainly, there are those who argue strongly that organizations face an inexorable tendency to treat even core people not just as a resource but also as contingent. Clarke (1998) maintains that the Aristotelian view of organizations as places where people self-actualize and are encouraged to develop will always be beaten by the 'utilitarianism of the boardroom' which has as a main priority '"the hard stuff": the numbers' (p. 47). This leads Clarke to suggest that a way forward is to 'explain openly that employees will ultimately be seen as costs, and that financial capital will always take precedence over intellectual capital' (p. 48). However, if organizations follow Clarke's advice the core are clearly being told that they are contingent. They do not enjoy a relationship with the organization. They are being offered a transaction that does not differ fundamentally from the transaction offered to the periphery.

Schein (1997) sees the pressure for this response as being exerted on and through CEOs. He says that 'CEOs the world over live in a financial environment in which their attention is focused primarily on the financial well being of their organization' (p. 5) and he goes on to describe how they 'are likely to have learned from their own experience and from fellow CEO's ... that people are a cost rather than an asset' (p. 5). A similar point is made by Ghoshal and Caulkin (1998). They argue that company boards ask CEOs to put 'above everything else' the fulfilment of their 'mission to capital markets'. This argument was borne out by Altman and Post's (1996) survey of senior executives of 25 Fortune 500 companies. The respondents suggested that shareholder demands for short-term profits were the main emphasis for executives and lead to cost cutting via employees.

Overall, there is clearly a great pressure to compromise the treatment of the core as a resource and to revert to treating it as a cost. This leads Donkin (1997a) to say it is 'simply not true' to describe people as the greatest asset of a company. Certainly, the mere labelling of a group of staff as core will not protect them from the pressures of also being a cost. They will be sent a mixed message from which there is only one conclusion: they are contingent. Sending a mixed message is precisely what organizations will find themselves doing unless they resist the forces to treat the core as a cost as well as a resource. Such resistance requires a very clear compartmentalization between the core and periphery and this is only likely to be maintained if there is a strategy to build and retain the core. Giving a clear message to the core also requires a strict consistency over time, across messengers and across members of the group. If this compartmentalization and consistency are not achieved, the message of low commitment will predominate and the organization trying to give both messages will end up in much the same position as if it had only given the message of people being contingent. Failing to recognize this will have consequences in both the long and short term. The long-term consequence is a result of the short-term effects. In the short term people will reciprocate the lack of commitment and leave. In the longer term, the firm will find it lacks a body of people ready to take on leadership positions.

## Message received: over and out

Whether or not organizations are meaning to convey mixed messages, there are those who argue that the core is receiving the message that they are a cost. In a survey of high-potential staff in the UK carried out in 1997, Holbeche (1998) found that many of her interviewees 'perceive messages about "manage your own career" to be an abdication of responsibility on the part of the employer' (p. 7). She also found that it led to mistrust that the employment relationship would be mutually beneficial.

The net result is that the core perceive themselves as only core for the time being. In particular, Herriot *et al.* (1998) observe that 'even among those to whom we thought we were giving sufficient security to engage their commitment and innovation, we find a marked degree of cynicism and mistrust of top management. The so-called core is crumbling' (p. 6). While these writers' description errs on the lurid, it is not necessary to look far to see why the core might doubt their status.

Yeung and McBride (1998) opened an article in the *Financial Times* of 23 September 1998, reminding their readers that 'last week, Vickers, the defence group announced it would cut 650 jobs in Leeds and Newcastle upon Tyne, and Shell said it would close its London headquarters, where 2000 people are employed. Yesterday, Barclaycard announced the loss of 1100 jobs.' It is hard to imagine that the 'core' of these companies was not affected. The result of the announcements is, say Yeung and McBride, that fear takes hold as well as short-term thinking. Unless these organizations handle the matter extremely carefully, which of course they might well do, they run the risk that 'headhunters will be lying in wait for managers with sound records, and "stars" who have not been reassured about their prospects may decide to jump ship rather than be pushed – even when the company never intended to off-load them'.

Aside from rounds of redundancies, some organizations exhibit a propensity to sack particular individuals, even those regarded as in the inner sanctum. This behaviour must also cause the core to pause for thought and wonder what 'core' means. The doubt is captured by O'Brien and Truell's (1998) headline 'At Citigroup, fears of exodus', which opens a report on how Citigroup's president was asked to resign. The reporters say this man was widely considered to be the heir apparent to the two co-chief executives and 'had once seemed more like a son' than an employee to one of them.

When people in the core witness either mass lay-offs from their ranks or the sacking of the heir apparent, they are bound to wonder when it will be their turn. They will receive a message that they are contingent even though such a message might not have been intended by the organization. Under these circumstances, they might choose to leave before they are pushed, as suggested by Yeung and McBride.

## PRESERVED BY A STRATEGY

It can be concluded that the split between the periphery and the core might well have been less than clean in many organizations. The core might have been sent the new psychological contract of contingency, thereby blurring the core–periphery distinction. Furthermore, even if not sent, the core group of staff might well have received some of the messages of changed psychological contracts that have applied to the periphery.

This might not be true of all organizations or all core staff. Nevertheless, it can be seen that there is a powerful tendency for the need for flexibility and cost cutting to assert itself and to overpower messages to people that they are a resource. It seems likely to be the dominant need for all organizations other than those that have a strategy to build a resource. Only in this case will the need for a resource have been considered against the need for flexibility and cost control and a decision taken to sacrifice the short term for the long term. Without a strategy, the option to have the core as a resource is likely to be overtaken by the need to treat them as a cost. The organization will behave expediently in the short term and send mixed messages to the core. Furthermore, it is only the existence of the strategy that will persuade the core that they are special. They have to see a clear and coherent strategy for their own recruitment, development and retention. Otherwise, the message that will be received is one of short-termism.

Yet, to commit to a strategy, as Pfeffer (1994) makes clear, requires overcoming an unfortunate paradox. 'If the organization is doing well, it may feel no need to worry about its competitive position. By the same token, if the organization is in financial distress, the immediate pressures may be too severe to embark on activities that provide productivity and profit advantages, but only after a longer, and unknown, period of time' (p. 55).

Perhaps it is a result of this paradox that a report by Patterson *et al.* (1997) for the UK's Institute of Personnel and Development (IPD) found that personnel strategies were a low priority for most of the companies it researched. In addition, as Ezzamel *et al.* (1996) observe, 'business strategy is frequently developed in advance of an HRM strategy or, at best, is loosely coupled to it' (p. 66). Under these circumstances, the existence and preservation of the core are unlikely to be on the agenda when business strategies are considered.

Organizations will only sacrifice the short term if the pursuit of the long-term gain is part of a business strategy. Furthermore, by its very nature, organizations will only sacrifice the short term if they consider the price of not doing so to be even greater than the sacrifice itself. This price revolves around the effects on staff of seeing themselves as subject to a contingent contract. If people sense they are a cost that could be pruned at short notice, they will stay only while the benefits from doing so outweigh the opportunities from leaving. The benefits of staying are the rewards of the immediate transaction. However, these benefits could cease at any time and not at a time of their choosing. The opportunities from leaving are obtaining either a better transaction or a more certain stream of transactions from an organization that offers a relationship. It is not hard to imagine the opportunities from leaving being more persuasive than the benefits of staying. If that is the case the core will quite likely take pre-emptive action and could leave at any time. At its crux, the argument is that if you fail to treat people as if they are wanted for the long term, they are unlikely to wait around even for the short term. The next chapter examines in greater detail the effect on the core if they have not been segregated successfully from the periphery, and have come to see them-selves more as a cost than a resource.

# If the core is contingent      5

If the need for cost cutting and flexibility is the dominant message received by the core, it will mean that they feel subject to the sense of contingency described in Chapter 2. People will see themselves as under a psychological contract of less commitment than in the past from the organization. This will be demonstrated most graphically by periodic episodes of 'decruitment' by 'denominator managers'. However, these episodes are only the eruption of the underlying attitude towards people. Both the episodes and the attitude will have their effects. Overall, and put simply, these effects are likely to add up to the undermining of the attempt to build a winning resource.

## THE AFTER-SHOCK OF DECRUITING

Clearly, one cannot set one's face against reality. Delayering has been inevitable in order to achieve responsiveness to the environment and, naturally, there will be occasions when any organization has to make staff redundant. At issue is how this is communicated and particularly whether laying people off is seen by staff as a knee-jerk reaction or a last resort. Delayering as it has frequently been carried out perversely loosens the very commitment of the newly empowered people in whom it is required. It has suggested to staff that their lay-offs are the first and an easy option while stockholders grow rich and senior management continue to enjoy 'fat cat' salaries. In addition, lay-offs and restructuring in some organizations have become a repeated reaction, and a failed solution, to the contemporary environment. To cap it all, with each round of redundancies, organizations have had to be decreasingly 'generous' with their severance terms (Altman and Post, 1996).

Under these circumstances, it seems inevitable that those working in downsizing organizations will wonder when their turn might come and that those who have been laid off and are in new employment will wonder whether their turn might come again. Hamel and Prahalad (1994) declare that 'one of the inevitable results of downsizing is plummeting employee

morale' (p. 11). They continue by saying 'the most talented people antici-
pate the carnage and flee for safety' (p. 23). Reichheld (1996) puts it
ironically, saying, 'a layoff rarely exhilarates employees. What it does do is
stifle creativity, discourage risk-taking, and destroy loyalty' (p. 95). In the
same vein, Altman and Post (1996) describe cuts in staff as undermining
trust, loyalty and commitment.

This phenomenon has been labelled 'survivor syndrome'. Armstrong-
Stassen (1998) discusses how the effects of downsizing can be
'devastating' on survivors, inducing in them as much stress as was
suffered by those who are laid off. She showed in her case study of lay-offs
in a Fortune 100 telecommunications company that those higher in the
organization perceived less procedural injustice about the way the lay-offs
were handled than those lower down. The senior people also had less
sense of powerlessness. Armstrong-Stassen speculates that senior people
might see greater fairness in the act of laying people off because they have
greater access to information on the company's lack of well-being. The
study suggests that senior people might not necessarily be in touch with
the same feelings as their staff about redundancies.

Apart from the respondent's level, Armstrong-Stassen found that the
perception of procedural injustice was related particularly to the period of
notice and help provided by the company to those laid off. As Altman and
Post (1996), have observed, this help diminishes with each round of
redundancies.

A further case study with related results is provided by Brockner, *et al.*
(1993). They report a field study of a chain of 773 stores in the USA. They
found that organizational commitment fell for those who had the strongest links with people who were laid off, and that this fall was especially
marked if the company was seen as having acted unfairly to the people
laid off.

Sennett (1998) also discusses how 'those who survive the process of re-
engineering may become as embittered as those who are fired' and he
suggests that 'this was IBM's experience in the Hudson Valley in the early
1990s'. Survivor syndrome also featured strongly in the UK's Institute of
Management survey of the attitudes of 1300 managers, reported by Houlder (1995). It painted a picture of 'overwork, stress and insecurity' and this
was said to be particularly acute for those left in organizations that had
had rounds of redundancies. Clay (1998) also describes the 'grave risks to
their mental and physical well-being' faced by the survivors of a round of
redundancies. Creating survivors out of them seems highly likely to
disrupt any attempt by the organization to build a resource on which it can
count. Reichheld (1996) suggests that the problem extends to most Fortune
500 companies. The effect is that 'mistrust and anxiety replace feelings of
loyalty and security' (p. 93). The Conference Board report adduces a good

deal of evidence on how the effect of downsizing has been to disrupt trust. As an example, they cite Gemini Consulting which downsized and how 'employees saw that retrenchment as a breach of trust' (p. 15).

The overall effect is summed up by Sims (1994) who describes how 'letting people go' 'profoundly affects the surviving employees. Some of their most basic tenets – beliefs in fairness, equity and justice – have been violated. . . . Company loyalty is quickly becoming extinct' (p. 374). Furthermore, he says, there is no reason to suppose this applies to just those people the organization is less bothered about, and suggests the phenomenon applies to all because survivor syndrome applies to all. Certainly, survivor syndrome will apply to the core if they do not see themselves as clearly separate from the group who suffered the lay-offs.

The effects of redundancies seem to be compounded when lay-offs occur in rounds. Simple common sense would encourage people to move to an organization with a better future. As Pfeffer (1998) says, in describing the four rounds of redundancies at Apple between 1985 and 1997, the effect was seen as 'making people unsure of their futures and tempting the best people to leave' (p. 25).

Inevitably there will be occasions when organizations have to lay people off. What is at issue is whether the lay-offs over the last two decades have been so extensive, applying as much to the core as anybody else, that the core see themselves as survivors rather than a strategic resource. Taken together, these studies suggest this might well be the case. The effect will be greater if the lay-offs are seen to have been handled badly or unfairly. This perception seems particularly likely among people who are junior in the organization, the people with potential.

## THE DRIPPING TAP OF FLEXIBILITY

Decruitment happens and then it is over. Probably having an even greater effect on staff is the broader ongoing attitude of organizations, of which lay-offs are but one manifestation. The attitude is one by which organizations have almost relished their lack of commitment. It can be seen as born from a desire by organizations to achieve flexibility in their contracts with people. The potential problem for organizations is the negative consequences of changing the career and security elements of the psychological contract. The change in the psychological contract is widely seen as leading to a lack of a sense of fairness and trust, which, in turn, leads to a lack of commitment by staff. Putting it baldly, Reichheld (1996) describes the policies of a lot of companies as having the effect to 'discourage or even destroy employee loyalty' (p. 92).

There is a good deal of evidence to support the link of the changing contract to the lack of commitment by staff. In order to examine it, the word 'commitment' needs some discussion. It is, like many words, one for which we think we know the meaning, until we start to examine it. Exhaustive reviews of the commitment literature are provided by Mathieu and Zajac (1990) and Meyer and Allen (1997). Mathieu and Zajac (1990) provide the general definition of commitment as 'a bond or linking of the individual to the organization' (p. 171) from which they separate two types of commitment. These two are:

- **Attitudinal**   This is an emotional identification with the organization

- **Calculated**   This is an instrumental identification, and is based on individuals perceiving that they cannot afford to leave. There is no practical alternative to the organization as a route for earning one's living

Meyer and Allen use the labels 'affective' and 'continuance' for these two types of commitment and add a third. This is 'normative' and refers to the sense of moral obligation and duty that ties a person to an organization.

Meyer and Allen relate commitment to the consequences of retention as well as to the productivity and well-being of staff. In turn, commitment is caused by a range of immediate (proximal) and background (distal) factors. Their full model is shown in Figure 5.1.

It can be seen that a major influence on people's commitment is their experience of fair treatment. Changing the career and security elements of the psychological contract has been associated with unfairness by Meyer and Allen and Kessler and Undy (1996). The change results in a lowering of affective commitment, relative to continuance commitment. Guest and Conway (1996, 1997) summarize the state of the psychological contract in terms of the 'fairness, trust and delivery of the deal' that the employee experiences. Like Meyer and Allen, they say it has several consequences apart from the attitude of commitment and the behavioural intention to stay or quit. The consequences are divided into two sets. First are the attitudes of commitment, job satisfaction and employment relations. Second are the behaviours of citizenship, shown by people making contributions beyond their role, motivation, effort and attendance/absence. According to Guest and Conway, the extent to which people experience feelings of fairness, trust and delivery depends upon organizational culture, perceived alternative employment, HR practices, and expectations, particularly of tenure, promotion and redundancy. Based on this analysis, sending the core a revised psychological contract about which they feel a lack of fairness, trust and delivery might well affect their commitment as well as their satisfaction and citizenship.

The link between the changed psychological contract and people's commitment is supported by Worrall and Cooper's (1997) survey. It suggests that organizational change has been accompanied by decreased security, morale, loyalty and motivation and that declines in security are at least correlated with decreased loyalty, morale and motivation.

There is, then, quite persuasive evidence that changes in the contract lessen people's commitment. While some changes to the contract were inevitable, it is not clear that they have been contained to an acceptable level or implemented in a manner that people see as reasonable. In particular, it is quite possible that the core have been treated in a way that will have lowered their commitment. The greatest change to the psychological contract is the introduction of the boundaryless career. Boundarylessness as an attitude by the organization seems bound to lessen people's sense of being offered a relationship. Paradoxically, this helps create the very rootlessness that the model then takes as its starting point. The way in which this happens is ably described by Mirvis and Hall (1996a). They say that under the new model some people can hope that they will 'move seamlessly across levels and functions, through different

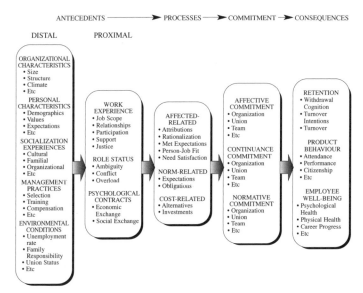

**Figure 5.1** A multidimensional model of organizational commitment, its antecedents, and its consequences. *Source*: J.P. Meyer and N.J. Allen, *Commitment in the workplace: Theory, research and application*, p. 106, copyright © 1997. Reprinted by permission of Sage Publications, Inc.

kinds of jobs, and even from company to company through a boundary-less career' (p. 238). However, they advise that many may find this impossible and that they will need to re-examine their career aspirations. If they do not do so, they will 'risk disappointment and a sense of failure' (p. 238).

Mirvis and Hall (1996a) suggest that responsibility for careers will increasingly fall on the individual because boundaryless organizations will be too uncertain to plan meaningfully a person's career. They say that, at present, 'the movement toward the boundaryless organization is well ahead of acceptance of the boundaryless career' (p. 250) and this has led to feelings of let-down and abandonment. These feelings are analogous to the feeling of being let down in a romantic relationship. People joined organizations thinking they had a future together, only to find that the organization is practising and urging a rather open relationship. They suggest that as boundaryless careers become more of the norm people will identify with their work rather than an organization and that their feeling about their relationship with the organization will be 'just "sex", not "marriage"' (p. 250).

Miles and Snow (1996) suggest that the career of the knowledge worker in the 'fourth-wave . . . may recapture many of the original characteristics of the classic professions' (p. 98). What they mean by this is that knowl-edge workers will be entirely their own masters and mistresses just like a barrister/lawyer or surgeon in private practice. They suggest that fourth-wave organizations will be minimalist and 'merely house and facilitate the activities of entrepreneurial professionals' (p. 108). In such cellular organi-zations people take full charge of their careers. The boundaryless career might now be an appropriate response to the high level of mobility by staff. However, it is a level of mobility that is partly created by organiza-tions which have persuaded themselves that boundarylessness is an ideal to strive for.

An interesting case study that illustrates these effects is provided by Pfeffer's (1998) description of events at Apple. Having been a tightly knit and collegiate company, Pfeffer describes how, in 1985, Apple pioneered the new employment contract. He says, 'consistently, and with increasing frequency over the years, the company maintained that its responsibility to its employees was not to give them any security or a career with a progression of jobs, but rather simply to provide a series of challenging job assignments that would permit employees to learn and develop and so to be readily employable' (p. 24). He describes how this policy that advo-cated boundarylessness, not surprisingly, encouraged people to be boundaryless. They tended to move on to other companies once they had developed talent and skills at Apple. Whatever the gains might be, boundaryless careers would seem clearly to carry a cost in terms of increasing the uncertainty that organizations face. Pfeffer's description also draws attention to the fact that the new contract at Apple occurred in parallel with a series of rounds of redundancies. Although the two do not inevitably occur together, it can safely be concluded that the new contract plus rounds of redundancies will have a magnified impact on people's commitment.


## FOOTLOOSE AND FANCY FREE

While imposing flexible contracts was an understandable response to general uncertainty, with this attitude organizations have 'liberated' professionals and given them the confidence to take charge of this type of contract. In many respects it can be argued that the emphasis by organizations on flexibility has created the attitudes of the knowledge worker. These attitudes are caricatured in the identity of Generation X. Certainly at the level of stereotype, the Generation X manager is said to 'believe you get better salaries and challenges not by waiting patiently to move up the ladder, but by moving between companies' (Summers, 1998). Applying the stereotype more comprehensively, Altman (1998) describes how members of Generation X witnessed 'the jobs of their parents' generation axed by rationalisation or delayering, and so neither want nor expect to spend their own working lives in a single organisation. They will work hard and put in long hours, but only for as long as it suits them, moving on once they have learnt what they can from an organisation' (p. 42). Much the same point is made by Douglas T. Hall and Associates (1996) in the preface to their book *The career is dead – long live the career*. Their argument is that careers are no longer organizational. They now belong to individuals who 'no longer expect – or, in many cases, want – a long-term career within a particular organization' (pp. xi–xii).

Research by King and Guest (1998) among the graduates in nine large organizations also suggest that the rhetoric has been taken up by staff. A common theme among the people interviewed was employability. The researchers found that working for a variety of companies was a strategy that these people used to gain a broad range of experience and achieve faster progression in terms of salary and grade than could result from staying with one company.

Similarly, the Conference Board (1997) notes that 'some employees take to the new rules with enthusiasm' (p. 13). They cite IBM as being among the companies that recognize that their fast-paced environment will tend to attract people for whom frequent job changes are not aversive. The report also cites the example of Philips in the Netherlands as a company where the majority of newer senior employees are quite used to having short-term contracts.

It can be seen that sending people the message of flexibility might have lessened their commitment, and that for some people this non-committal relationship is one that suits them well. On the face of it, organizations have moved these people two strides away from being a resource upon which they can rely. In one stride, the organization loosened its commitment. In the second, people came not to want it. Nowadays, organizations have to beat the temptation presented to their staff to click into such dens of choice as the *Wall Street Journal's* interactive free site at http:careers.wsj.com. The *Wall Street Journal* describes how the site represents top-level career opportunities and enables people to search for positions as well as getting tips on improving their résumé. Now, it is the knowledge workers who are as non-committal as they want to be.

In many respects organizations have more to lose from this change than their staff. As Weick (1996) notes, organizations might need knowledge workers more than knowledge workers need organizations. Organizations still need people who are capable. It is quite possible that a significant proportion of these people who used to be motivated by a career within an organization and a sense of security have now found they can do quite well operating independently of an organization. They have followed the implicit advice of Bridges (1998) to form You and Co., self-analysing on the way their DATA (desire, abilities, temperament and assets). Showing a general air of confidence, Guest and Conway (1997) report that 57 per cent of the sample they surveyed were either 'very or somewhat confident that they would be able to find another job as good as their present one without too much difficulty' (p. 14).

In other words, it is possible that people have adjusted to the new realities, feel quite confident of themselves and have become highly mobile. Many have now got used to the new realities. It is not perhaps too fanciful to make use of the original simile of paternalism to liken the transition to being forced to leave home and to come to terms with a new-found independence. In Hall's (1996) view the contemporary career involves having a contract that is 'more with oneself, in connection to other people, and with one's work, and less with the organization' (p. 343).

Having thus liberated knowledge workers, it is now apparent to firms that they might have created a problem for themselves. To sit beside the knowledge worker, organizations are now appointing knowledge officers, responsible for the husbandry of knowledge in the organization. As Donkin (1998d) observes, the knowledge officer has an interest that is diametrically opposite to that of the knowledge worker 'who is unwilling to share his know-how'.

In summary, while the move from a paternalistic bond has many positive aspects for employers, such as increasing people's sense of responsibility and emphasizing the need to deliver results, it runs the danger from the employer's point of view that they have created additional uncertainty for themselves. In particular, it has made it less certain whether their high-potential staff will still be with them in the near term, let alone through to the stage when they would reach the maturity to take on the leadership role. At the very least, it is naive to assume that the message of employability will be received passively by staff who will wait until they are no longer needed. There is no reason to suppose that their timing will suit their employers. This uncertainty then forms part of the changing environment to which employers must respond. As Pfeffer (1998) puts it, 'having told people that they need to be "career self-reliant" and having provided them with the necessary resources, the companies are then surprised when they face the very turnover that their programs have helped foster' (p. 163). The main links leading to this turnover are shown in Figure 5.2.

## A CHAIN REACTION

Although some knowledge workers might have taken to their liberation, they can still be expected to prefer to go to work for 'good' employers. Offered the choice, presumably, they will go to the organization that has a reputation of sticking by people, rather than one that has the name of being a 'hire them, fire them' employer. Talented people can be choosy people. Imposing contingency on the core might not only loosen the

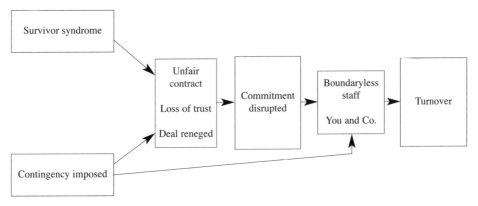

**Figure 5.2** Releasing the core

commitment of existing staff. It could make it difficult to get new talent when it is needed. For example, Mirvis and Hall (1996a) note that companies that acquire a bad reputation have difficulty recruiting people in a subsequent 'boom'.

## AN ALTERNATIVE READING

The linkages leading to a lack of commitment and 'liberated' knowledge workers seem clear. They will be triggered if the need by organizations for flexibility competes with the need to have people as a resource. The need for flexibility will dominate. This state of competition will prevail unless there is a clear strategy to treat people as a resource and enter into a relationship with them rather than a transaction. Transactions provide flexibility, but the evidence suggests they will have the undesirable consequence of a failure to retain knowledge workers.

There is, however, an alternative reading. This acknowledges that the psychological contract has altered for core staff so that they are now subject to a transaction rather than a relationship. However, the transaction is assumed to give people all they want. This seems to be the view of Mirvis and Hall (1996a) who describe how 'companies who have taken a lead in responding to new conditions facing their business typically invest more in employee development and do more to retain their people' (p. 251). They go on to suggest companies will stipulate that people must be prepared to make lateral moves and to take responsibility for developing themselves and their careers. In other words, Mirvis and Hall seem to see the new deal as not necessarily leading to unwanted results. Perhaps, organizations have found a way forward and can both recruit and retain people by offering a transaction. This seems to be the opinion of some of the executives interviewed by Altman and Post (1996) who report that the emphasis on performance has helped recruit and retain high performers. However, transactions have a day-to-day quality and do not convey any sense of securing the resource upon whom the organization's long-term future depends. The next chapter examines the evidence of whether the contract with the core is actually working perfectly satisfactorily or whether there is a problem that needs to be rectified.

# Shreds of evidence    6

Evidence is needed to help decide which of three readings is most accurate. Organizations might be having difficulty building and retaining the core as a result of the move from a relationship to a transaction. Alternatively, they might have put together transactions that work: the exchange of knowledge work for employability might be one that retains the knowledge worker's services. Finally, organizations might have continued to enjoy perfectly good relationships with their core. They might have maintained an adequate separation between their core and periphery, rather than allowing the need for contingency and transactions to permeate to the core. If everything to do with knowledge workers, in terms of their satisfaction and plans to stay, is found to be fine, then, presumably, organizations have built perfectly good relationships with them or at least they have found transactions that work.

The initial evidence might seem quite positive. Certainly, anything wrong might not be self-evident to the CEO who sees a booming stock price and general 'good news' on the health of the business. If there are any problems on the human resources (HR) front, the CEO might reason, they are not sufficient to be having an impact and are probably not worth worrying about. However, it is worth the CEO taking a deeper look because it is just possible that behind the good news of the quarterly results lies the bad news concerning the core human resource. Perhaps, organizations do not have a manifest problem at present, but behind the good news of higher earnings per share bought by delayerings and mergers there might lie the potential bad news of staff with lessened commitment and loyalty. It is the HR equivalent of living off capital. Future growth based upon the intellectual capital of a committed core of knowledge workers will be harder to achieve.

## WHO WANTS TO LEAVE?

The first type of evidence concerns whether high potential staff are tending towards or away from being basically committed as well as motivated and content. There are numerous tales from both sides of the Atlantic of how bad everyone feels in organizations. For example, Herriot and Pemberton (1995) introduce their book on the 'new deals' imposed on managers by saying that 'the assurance of a secure future for individuals and their families has crumbled away' (p. xiii). The problem with such descriptions is that they seem entirely based on the impressions of the people writing them, most of whom are consultants. In turn, these consultants might well have been exposed to more problematic organizations rather than typical organizations. It is like asking a group of doctors about the health of the nation, or lawyers about its honesty. The impressions need support from survey data.

Turning to the evidence, Pickard (1997a) reports a survey of UK graduates that revealed a disparity between what people want and what they receive. The survey showed that three-quarters or more graduates look for three factors – good training, good career prospects and job security – in choosing their employer. However only 39 per cent were satisfied with their training and just 25 per cent with career prospects and 20 per cent with security.

The above percentage for satisfaction with security stands in marked contrast to a survey, also UK-based, by Guest and Conway (1996). They found 'a surprising degree of employment security' (p. 16) which they contrast with 'the assertions by some commentators that employees have accepted a new reality by abandoning their loyalty and giving up on the idea of a career' (p. 16). Repeating their survey a year later, these same authors (Guest and Conway, 1997) are moved to conclude that 'worries about redundancy and job insecurity are, at least temporarily, a thing of the past' (p. 13). They also observe that 'across the issues of fairness, trust and delivery of the deal, employees are overwhelmingly positive' (p. 16). They state that 'worries about job security are confined to a minority of the working population' (p. 23). Indeed, these authors found that 42 per cent felt more secure than a year before, with 22 per cent feeling less secure.

Guest and Conway's results seem to stand in the face of the findings in the same year by Worrall and Cooper (1997). They describe how 'the restructuring that has taken place in UK businesses over the last 12 months has had a massively negative effect on employee loyalty, morale, motivation and perceptions of job security' (p. 33). The results were replicated a year later in a further survey by Worrall and Cooper (1998). In both years, Worrall and Cooper found the negative effects of change to be particularly profound in public limited companies and in the public sector.

The consequences of which survey paints the more accurate picture is clearly important in finding a way forward. If Guest and Conway are correct then it would seem that organizations have good relational contracts with their core. On the other hand, if Worrall and Cooper are correct, then it appears that organizations have not only tended to move to transactional contracts with staff, but also that only small majorities and sometimes minorities of people find the elements of the exchange satisfactory. Details are shown in Table 6.1. It refers to the entire Worrall and Cooper (1998) sample and shows, by managerial level, the differences between the percentage who are satisfied and the percentage who are dissatisfied with aspects of the present job. For example, 11 per cent more middle managers are satisfied than dissatisfied with job security. Five per cent more are dissatisfied than satisfied with career opportunities.

One explanation for the contrast between the Guest and Conway surveys and those by Worrall and Cooper might lie in the organizations they have sampled. Perhaps Guest and Conway happened upon organizations that were doing the right things and Worrall and Cooper chose those less gifted in staff management. However, this seems a rather unlikely possibility. Alternatively, perhaps it depends on whom they asked. Supporting this interpretation, Worrall and Cooper (1997) found that responses were strongly related to the respondent's level in the organization, with a discontinuity between directors and senior managers. This is shown in Table 6.1. It was also evident that those in the boardroom had far less perception of a drop in overall employee loyalty, morale, motivation and job security as a result of restructuring than did people below board

**Table 6.1**  Net satisfaction with aspects of present job by managerial level (%)

| Base: 1312 respondents | All | Chair/ CE/MD | Director | Senior manager | Middle manager | Junior manager |
|---|---|---|---|---|---|---|
| Relationship with peers | 75 | 73 | 72 | 76 | 76 | 71 |
| Relationship with boss | 49 | 53 | 54 | 50 | 47 | 42 |
| Level of autonomy | 48 | 79 | 67 | 49 | 32 | 26 |
| Training opportunities | 26 | 38 | 29 | 30 | 23 | 4 |
| Job security | 21 | 46 | 35 | 18 | 11 | 9 |
| Reward and remuneration | 20 | 38 | 34 | 27 | 8 | −8 |
| Downward communications | 18 | 57 | 40 | 19 | 6 | −8 |
| Career opportunities | 17 | 66 | 43 | 14 | −5 | −14 |
| Recognition for performance | 16 | 52 | 37 | 15 | 4 | −12 |
| Feedback | 10 | 45 | 28 | 9 | −2 | −13 |
| Workload | −2 | 13 | 1 | −6 | −5 | −10 |

level. Indeed board members tended to see these variables as having improved, whereas those below the board saw them as having suffered.

The difference in perceptions becomes even more extreme in answers to a mix of questions dealing with both the respondent's own feelings (e.g. 'I often think about leaving my organisation') and feelings about the organization as a whole (e.g. 'Morale is good overall in my organisation'). These questions were asked of both people who had experienced a restructuring and those who had not. Again the discontinuity was between the board and those below the board. For example, a majority of those below the board affirmed that they often think about leaving the organization, whereas it was a minority of people at board level. In addition, chairpersons were 'massively more positive' than junior managers about morale in the organization. Finally, a minority of those below the board concurred that 'my organisation will provide me with a secure job for the foreseeable future' whereas it was endorsed by a majority of those at board level.

The finding of different perceptions links with Armstrong-Stassen's (1998) results discussed in Chapter 5 and is clearly one which boards should take extremely seriously. In particular, they should not ask themselves about morale in the organization. They should ask their staff. It is possible that these differences in perception provide part of the explanation for the different results obtained by Guest and Conway on the one hand and Worrall and Cooper on the other. However, it can be only a partial explanation because under half of Guest and Conway's sample graded themselves as management.

The remainder of the explanation for the different findings might be that Guest and Conway (1997) are rather complacent in their conclusions. Although they are generally very upbeat, they found only 36 per cent had never thought about leaving their job, with 18 per cent having looked around for other jobs and 11 per cent currently trying to leave. Whether this is good or bad news seems open to interpretation. In addition, the findings on commitment, measured by loyalty and pride, might not be interpreted as positively as they are by Guest and Conway (1997) themselves. Just over half their sample felt 'some loyalty' or less, in contrast to the other half who felt 'a lot of loyalty'. Clearly, much turns on people's interpretation of 'some', but the spin that could be put on the finding might be in terms of 50 per cent of people feeling only 'some' loyalty. They also found that 70 per cent felt only 'quite' proud to tell people the organization they worked for.

Guest and Conway (1997) also ignore an apparent contradiction in their results. They found Britain to be 'a nation working extremely hard' and they also found that 'only 35 per cent feel very motivated in their job' (p. 29). Later, they comment that 'while motivation is associated with a positive psychological contract, high effort is associated with a poorer psychological contract' (p. 35). On the face of it, their findings of the nation's overall hard work and not particularly high motivation appear to sit unhappily with the contention that the psychological contract is extremely positive.

If consistent results cannot be obtained within a country, it makes it extremely difficult to interpret any differences that are found between countries. Any national differences might simply be due to sampling 'errors'. With that caveat, it is interesting to note that the Conference Board (1997) suggests that morale problems might be greater in the USA than elsewhere. Across nations, they found 58 per cent of companies having such problems, but they note that this percentage is 71 for the USA in contrast to 30 elsewhere. Likewise trust is mentioned as a problem by 73 per cent in the USA and 47 per cent elsewhere.

Given the equivocal nature of the results of these surveys, the best way forward must be to find out the picture in your particular organization. In terms of building a resource, the key questions are to do with people's sense of loyalty, commitment and intention to stay. People might feel better or worse in your organization than average. You might have been more or less successful than the average organization in insulating the core and in giving them the unequivocal message that they are resource. Or you might not. The only way to find out is to find out. It is, however, clear that you need to ask some straight questions and listen carefully to the answers. Worrall and Cooper's survey shows that those at the top tend to have a far rosier view than those whom they lead. The information you gather will be valuable, and give an overall sense of whether people stay because they want to or because they have to. However, it is also vital to observe what people do as well as what they say. They might claim to be content but still leave.

## IS EVERYBODY ACTING HAPPY?

Holbeche (1998) found in her survey of high-flyers in the UK that they do not give the impression that they are 'job hoppers'. She reports that nearly a third of people had been with their employer for 11 or more years and that a quarter had stayed with the organization that first employed them. She sees this as 'suggesting that, in the past at least, succession planning has been successful at developing and retaining key people within the organisation' (p. 18). On the other hand, evidence to suggest that the core is not sticking comes from Reichheld (1996) who reports that on average, Harvard MBAs change employers three to four times in their first 10 years out of school.

There are huge differences between organizations. Prickett (1998d) reports a survey showing that while one-tenth of employers had lost only 14 per cent of their 1993 recruits, another tenth had seen a full 96 per cent leave by the date of the survey. It is possible that those achieving the higher retention were in a different sector from the tenth suffering the near-total turnover and that different norms applied to staff in each sector. For example, from our consultancy experience, the finance sector has a far higher turnover than the public sector. Nevertheless, this seems unlikely to be the full explanation and, within a sector, an organization with lower turnover would appear at a clear advantage over others in winning a talent war. Such an organization is managing to build and retain talent rather than to lose the talented people who should bring it success in the future.

As with the issue of people's feelings, it is clearly important to check what is happening in your particular organization. At the very least, if the answer is that you are part of the high turnover group, it suggests that you need to review your strategy to win the talent war. The transactions you offer would not seem to be retaining people and you would be advised to consider joining those organizations that are looking to have a relationship with their core.

## DARKENING SKIES

Evidence on whether people generally are wanting to leave and evidence on whether they are actually leaving seems equivocal. However, it is clear, for example from Prickett (1998d), that there are huge differences between organizations in terms of the ability to retain people. It is also the case that there are troubling signs that are beginning to emerge. These signs suggest that the effects of liberating the knowledge worker are beginning to be felt generally across organizations. Notwithstanding the differences between organizations, issues of retention are becoming more prominent. Certainly, if America sets trends, it is important to heed the Conference Board (1997) report. It shows that high turnover is a relatively minor issue elsewhere, but is mentioned by 37 per cent of US companies as a concern.

Perhaps foreseeing the general problem of retaining people without a relational contract, Arthur and Rousseau (1996) ask whether the change to boundaryless careers is the paradigm shift as foretold by futurists or whether it is a temporary phenomenon which will be corrected as firms take back greater custody of people's careers. Certainly, there is an increasing number of reports suggesting that the wheel may be turning back towards treating people as a resource.

## TURNING THE CIRCLE

Welch (1998b) reports that the British bank Lloyds/TSB has brought in a new 'employee proposition' which their head of resourcing and planning is quoted as describing as 'a fancy way of saying a new psychological contract'. The bank 'has promised its employees jobs for life – if they can prove that they can adapt to change'.

Altman and Post (1996) describe how their survey of senior executives in 25 Fortune 500 companies revealed the opinion that the pendulum might have swung too far in favour of treating people as economic costs, leading the authors to declare that 'the pendulum is starting to swing back' (p. 67). The executives were looking for a contract that 'integrates the benefits of a more independent and flexible workforce with one that has some relational ties' (p. 65). Further evidence of a change of attitude towards people is contained in the report by Walsh (1998) on the dismissal of Al Dunlap by Sunbeam. Described as revelling in the nicknames 'Chainsaw Al and Rambo in Pinstripes', his approach was to cut thousands of jobs, yet the 'firm's profits and share price plummeted'. Employees were said to be 'celebrating'.

Research by Guest *et al.* (1998) among UK employers also suggested that some organizations 'were reverting to traditional contracts in some areas' (p. 194). Guest and Mackenzie Davey (1996) also report a move back to the 'traditional career' among the organizations taking part in the Career Research Forum, which is made up of 33 leading UK organizations.

Finally, Lancaster (1998) tells his *Wall Street Journal* readers that 'companies that once bragged about their re-engineered work processes and new quality measurements now are extolling the importance of human beings. They want to hire them, retain them, develop them and pay them gobs of money.'

The problem is that, as we have seen, employees themselves have moved on psychologically and the original contract no longer has the hold it might once have done. Employees are boundaryless. Holbeche (1998) reports that 80 per cent of people in her survey saw themselves alone as responsible for managing their careers. As Holbeche comments, these people's confidence is increased by their awareness that they are employable. She goes on to describe a more 'adult–adult relationship' which is based on the knowledge worker's power 'to make demands of the organisation which go beyond pay and rations' (p. 7). She also notes the great irony that 'the very skills which employers are looking for – such as the ability to get things done, to be innovative, customer oriented etc. – are precisely the skills which will help people get jobs elsewhere' (p. 7). It also helps them start their own companies. Eggers (1995) observes that start-up companies are being formed at what seems to be an ever-increasing rate by people who are disillusioned with or displaced by Fortune 500 companies.

The irony recorded by Holbeche is also noted by the Conference Board (1997). It concludes its survey on the new employment compact by asking: 'How will companies keep their top talent when managing one's own career is a key tenet of the new employment compact?' (p. 18). It is a key question and reflects the fact that organizations have changed the context of the employment relationship. Security is less of an issue for high potential people both in comparison to the past and in comparison to people of lesser talent.

We arrive, then, at a point where organizations might well have imparted to their core some of the same sense of contingency that applies to the periphery. Clearly, this does not apply to all organizations. Some will have been more successful than others at maintaining the distinction between the core and periphery and at offering the core the right relationship. However, this will only have been achieved by having the relationship as a strategy. Otherwise the expediency of day-to-day results will have prompted the organization to abandon the relationship in favour of transactions. While the evidence is mixed, there is a good argument for, at least, asking whether the transaction approach is not contributing to problems of retention and undermining efforts to build a talent base. Organizations would be well advised to consider whether they should subscribe to a strategy to woo back the affections of core staff and encourage them to stay longer.

# Finding a third way  7

## NOT GOING FORWARDS MEANS GOING BACKWARDS

Aside from answering the need for people as a resource, having a strategy also implies having taken account of the need for the organization to be responsive to change. The nature of the environment described in Chapter 1 must clearly be taken as given and the response in terms of organizations generally becoming and remaining more flexible is a necessity.

The twin needs to have a resource of talented people and for the organization to be responsive to change must be properly considered. A way forward must be found that meets them both. A third way is required. Otherwise, as Chapter 4 suggested, the organization will stumble between the needs, the message of contingency will dominate and the organization will risk losing its resource of talented people. If people sense they are a cost that could be pruned at any time, there is no reason to stay. They should leave when it suits them.

An organization needs to have a strategy that treats people as a resource if it is to move forwards and build and retain people for the long term. Otherwise, the message that will be received is one of short-termism. This could easily take the organization backwards. The absence of a strategy or trying to treat people ambivalently as a cost alongside treating them as a resource runs the real risk of creating a doubt in people's minds and encouraging them to move somewhere more certain which offers greater faith in the future. The long-term strategy is needed not just to move you forwards, but also to stop you moving backwards.

## SPECIFYING THE OBJECTIVES

A strategy to meet the need for people as a resource has twin goals. They are acquiring talented people and retaining talented people. Both will be served by the same strategy. The type of organization that retains talented people will be the type that people want to work for. It will gain a good reputation as an employer.

People's retention is inextricably linked to their commitment. McCaul *et al.* (1995) carried out a study from which they conclude that commitment is a global attitude towards the organization that includes people's intention to stay. Looking at the converse, Mathieu and Zajac's (1990) literature search demonstrated that lack of commitment was strongly correlated with people's intention to search for job alternatives (the correlation was 0.6) and intention to leave one's job (0.5). A more modest correlation was found with turnover (0.3), but that is not surprising since not everyone who wants to leave can do so.

Meyer and Allen (1997) also describe the link between commitment and intention to stay as well-established and say that it applies to all three forms of commitment (affective, continuance and normative). Meyer and Allen warn against the ethnocentric conclusion that affective commitment is the most desirable form. They say this might be true for North America but other cultures might put emphasis on the other types of commitment. Nevertheless, the benefit of affective commitment is that it is accompanied by a positive motivation, in contrast at least with continuance commitment which is both more grudging and unlikely to bind talented people who have the choice to move on. Furthermore, it seems unlikely that organizations can solve their retention problems by inducing the guilt associated with normative commitment. The strategy must be to concentrate on gaining people's affective commitment. It means getting people to feel an emotional attachment to the organization. The attachment is not just to particular colleagues or a manager. It needs to be to the organization as a whole, as represented by a culture and value system. In particular, it is to the organization as a satisfier of people's wants and in whose service they are applying their competencies. People need to see the organization as one they want to be part of. They need to see the organization as one they want to transact with. People do not just engage in transactions because they are on offer. They choose to transact. For this commitment, people will have to feel trust in the organization.

## CATERING FOR CHANGE

People's attachment and trust have to be gained within the context that there can be no guarantee of security from the employer. There cannot be a harking back to the 'good old days' of certainty and stability. Although it might have retained people, the old relationship was, at worst, paternalistic. At the very least, this paternalism has been replaced by a more realistic and businesslike exchange, involving the acceptance of mutual responsibility (Conference Board, 1997). Anyway, security is nowadays an empty promise. The promise of utter security is built on a lie. It needs to be replaced by a promise that can be fulfilled. Otherwise, trust will be lost as promises are continually rebroken. Indeed, as Heron (1998) points out, 'the truth is that there probably never was such a thing as a job for life' (p. 6). All that there used to be was 'a great deal more certainty about how your job was to be performed' (p. 6).

Employment clearly cannot be guaranteed and the absence of stability is the fundamental context for a strategy to build a resource. The strategy has to recognize the reality that, for example, the organization might be taken over by another. Being acquired by another company frequently results in a significant reduction in the workforce and the core are as vulnerable as the periphery to the fall-out from a merger or acquisition. In these circumstances, some degree of insecurity is now an obvious fact of organizational life. A strategy to retain people has to recognize this rather than make guarantees of security that cannot be delivered.

Quite apart from security being impossible to deliver, it is unlikely that organizations will find people with a high need for either security or stability as being suitable recruits to their core staff. The old deal might well have attracted such people to large and apparently dependable organizations that would offer a paternalistic contract. For example, a decade ago security was the most prominent career anchor of the managerial staff of a UK clearing bank with which we worked as consultants. The staff of another referred to it as 'mother bank'. People with such needs and attitudes are probably not those whom organizations nowadays wish to put in their high potential group. The organization has to be responsive to the environment and to be able to change. These are circumstances that seem unlikely to suit people who need a high level of security provided by other people and their environment. However, choosing people who will feel relatively untroubled in a context of change is very different from making those same people feel contingent. They should be able to engage with change and it is this very ability that means the organization will want a relationship with them and not a contingent transaction. It is also this quality that will enable them to leave if they feel put upon.

We arrive, then, at another paradox. The organization needs to secure the services of people who do not have a high need for security. To decide who these people might be, one might speculate with a line of thinking based on attachment theory. On the face of it, people without a high need for security might be those who feel secure.

There is a huge literature on people's sense of security, based around the attachment theory of Bowlby (1973). Following Bowlby, the categorization of people has been developed by Bartholomew and Horowitz (1991) into a fourfold choice which can be summarized by saying that people appear to be either:

- **Secure**   These people feel secure in themselves and are comfortable making commitments

- **Anxious ambivalent**   These people have a high need for reassurance

- **Avoidant**   These people avoid committed relationships and are subdivided into:

  - **Fearful avoidant**   They keep away from relationships because they do not want the pain that might be involved

  - **Dismissive avoidant**   They see no need for intense relationships with other people

Attachment styles are based on history. The less secure person is less secure for a reason. The problem for the insecure is that once their view of the world as a less 'safe' place has been set up, it perpetuates itself. People build up 'working models' of the world and use these as a guide to their interactions with the world. Once it is established in a working model, a person's attachment style tends to be a self-fulfilling prophecy. People behave towards the world in a way that begets behaviour from the world that only serves to confirm their view. The anxious-ambivalent person behaves anxious-ambivalently and this evokes responses from others that reinforce the anxious-ambivalent person's view of the world as a risky place. They also interpret behaviour from the world in a way that is congruent with their view. The secure person does not even perceive the threat in another's actions which is seen by the insecure.

These differences have been applied particularly to children's relationships with their parents and other attachment figures and extended to adult romantic relationships. There have also been speculative extensions of attachment theory into employment relationships (Feeney and Noller, 1996). It seems reasonable to suppose that attachment styles will generalize and carry forward into the workplace. The secure person might behave in a less edgy way towards others at work and perceive less sinister motives in their actions. The anxious-ambivalent and avoidant person might behave in an insecure way that others tire of. Such people are unlikely to have those competencies which are summed up by the vogue expression 'emotional intelligence' (Goleman, 1998). They get passed over for positions involving high levels of interpersonal skills.

Although people's working models of organizations might be born from and correlated with their working models of other people generally, the two models could separate. A person who is secure in interpersonal relationships might have employment experiences that, quite accurately, lead to the view that organizations cannot be trusted. Another person who is quite anxious with other people might learn to be quite secure within the world of work. In this way, there might come about a separation of the *interpersonal* and *organizational* attachment styles. People start their careers with an *interpersonal* attachment style. The interpersonal style that people bring to work seems likely to form the basis for their *organizational* attachment style. How the organizational style develops will depend upon how they are treated.

In terms of shaping a strategy to build and retain a core, organizations will be particularly concerned with the person's organizational attachment style. They will want to have people with secure attachments in their core. These people will have a sense of confidence in their career survival within the organization and be well placed to deal with change and uncertainty without experiencing the anxiety of the anxious-ambivalent person. The secure person is able to deal with insecurity. They have a sense of security while recognizing the uncertainties of the world. This is not necessarily any more of a conjuring trick than the interpersonally secure person's security in a world where relationships end and we all die. The organizational security seems likely to come from a mixture of belief in one's own career survival, together with belief in the support of the organization. Both beliefs need to be built up by the organization.

At this point it is helpful to introduce Rousseau and Wade-Benzoni's (1995) distinction between insiders who are core and those who are 'careerists' and 'jugglers'. Core staff are attached to the organization. By contrast, jugglers do not hold employment as a central life interest and careerists are short-term insiders who have as a priority their advancement within an industry or profession. They are true portfolio workers who go to the highest bidder. Within the organizational attachment model, careerists can be seen as those who started out employment as avoidant or who became that way. People who are avoidant cope with insecurity by self-sufficiency.

The organization needs to foster a strategy for enabling core staff to be organizationally secure. It needs to build their security by offering commitment. Otherwise, they will become careerists or jugglers. Ideally, the organization will be maintaining the working model of people who are already secure. Those who have become organizationally anxious-ambivalent or avoidant might be moved back to security, but this entails changing their model of the world and winning back their trust. Ideally also, the strategy will be directed at people who have a positive self-concept and who are, generally, risk-tolerant. Both of these factors were found by Judge *et al.* (1999) to be related to coping with change.

The strategy, then, needs to offer commitment to build the core's sense of being secure. This enables them both to handle the reality of uncertainty and to cope effectively with change, which serves to reinforce the organization's ability to make a commitment to them. A virtuous circle is set up as shown in Figure 7.1.

Trust and security are clearly related concepts. However, they are also subtly different. In the interpersonal context, trust is defined by Sorrentino *et al.* (1995) as the antithesis of doubt, encompassing a sense of confidence or conviction that the other person can be counted on to reciprocate positive feelings and respond to one's needs. Mikulincer (1998), describes trust as 'an integral part of secure attachment' (p. 1209). From his research he reports that 'for secure persons, the sense of trust was found to be exclusively related to the goal of intimacy in a relationship' (p. 1219). This is in contrast to the goal of security pursued by the anxious-ambivalent person and the goal of control that marks out the avoidant person. Mikulincer also describes how secure people deal with a violation of trust by engaging in constructive actions and turning to others for support. On the other hand, the anxious-ambivalent become hypervigilant and avoidant persons try to avoid confrontation.

Like attachment theory, this description of trust appears capable of extension to trust in organizations. In an organizational setting, intimacy can be translated into commitment. Commitment is the goal of the secure person, whereas security is the goal of the anxious-ambivalent and control is the aim of the avoidant. Commitment is what organizations want, yet

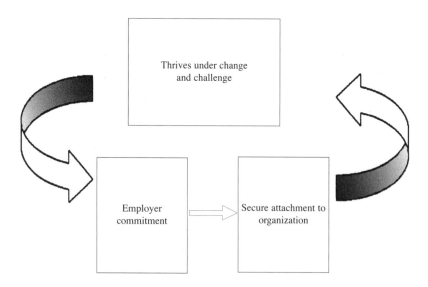

**Figure 7.1** Commitment enables change

they have been in danger of offering a deal that disrupts trust and serves only to reinforce the model of the world used by the avoidant. A continual emphasis on employability outside the organization is, on the face of it, not the psychological contract that builds a secure model of the world nor the contract that secure people want. What they want is commitment and this means being offered a relational contract.

## TRUST AND LEARNING

Trust requires the organization's commitment, but it also enables that commitment. It sets up another virtuous circle, as illustrated in Figure 7.2.

If the organization is to show a long-term commitment, people will have to adapt and learn. Goyder (1998) sums up the argument well when he describes the 'paradox of permanence' (p. 116). This is that survival requires adaptation, but it also requires 'something solid and unchanging' (p. 116). A hard core of people is required who will be permanent by being adaptable. By learning, they will continue to be suited to the changing environment. Learning requires trust. Webber (1993) describes how learning involves conversation. In order for there to be conversation, there has

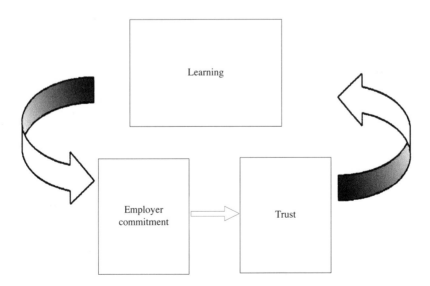

**Figure 7.2** Commitment enables learning

to be trust. The conversation to do with learning deals with people's experiences as well as their emotions. People have to feel sufficiently secure to be prepared to say what is really on their minds and to expose their ignorance and ask for help.

As Webber says, specifying trust is one thing; establishing it is another. He says it is 'tough because it is always linked to vulnerability, conflict and ambiguity' (p. 41) and the 'ultimate ambiguity that comes with managing on trust is the ambiguity of outcomes' (p. 42). In particular, there is 'no promise that the car won't leave the tracks or lose some passengers along the way' (p. 42). In summary, the organization needs to establish the commitment and trust of people who are comfortable with the uncertainty implicit in today's environment. To do so, it must show commitment and establish its trustworthiness.

## GAINING PEOPLE'S COMMITMENT AND TRUST

Commitment, together with trust and accountability, were the qualities that the Conference Board (1997) report found managers wanted in their staff. These were the three most cited qualities that employers considered most critical to the organization. Yet, the same report suggests that their priority is not reflected in the actions that firms are taking in their current HR initiatives. It states that only a half or less of initiatives are working on strengthening these critical behaviours. The report speculates that the reasons might be that firms regard trust and commitment as difficult to address with a single initiative. This must surely be true. It requires not an initiative but a long-term campaign to gain commitment and trust. Above all, it involves showing commitment by offering a relational contract. With the relational contract, commitment will be obtained from people by showing commitment to them. As Cooper (1997) aptly puts it, 'individuals may question their need to commit to organizations that do not commit to them' (p. 10). Similarly, Gaertner and Nollen (1989) conclude, 'psychological commitment is higher among employees who believe they are being treated as resources to be developed rather than commodities to buy and sell' (p. 987). The reason, says Pfeffer (1998), is 'the norm of reciprocity'. He describes it as 'truly a ubiquitous rule of behavior. ... Commitment is reciprocal. It is difficult to think of situations, at least in healthy, adult relationships, in which one side is committed and the other is not' (p. 181). Outside the employment relationship, Pfeffer suggests that people would 'think you are nuts' (p. 181) if you asked for a commitment with the proposal not to reciprocate.

However, organizations seem to have a rather half-hearted way of offering commitment. The Conference Board (1997) reports how Amoco's executives toured the world with the intention of demonstrating that the company's relationship with its employees is a reciprocal one involving commitments by both parties. Amoco show their commitment by ensuring people's employability. This will give employees the 'skills and experiences to compete for jobs external to Amoco as well as internally' (p. 16). The objective is to regain trust and commitment in the organization. However, the message surely has to be handled extremely carefully. Otherwise the message received might be the opposite to that intended. An emphasis on being made employable might be taken to suggest that one does not have a long-term future in the organization. It might disrupt trust.

Instead of emphasizing employability, organizations might be better off showing their commitment by valuing people, making clear the commitment is long-term, and treating them with honesty. All three have the desired consequence of gaining people's commitment and establishing them as a winning resource. Figure 7.3 sets out the approach.

## Valuing people

To show commitment and be trusted the organization needs to feel commitment. Otherwise it will be found out as a fraud. The first stage therefore is *believing* in the crucial importance of people. Gratton (1997) describes how Hewlett-Packard has built the commitment of its employees by having a set of values that 'places concern and respect for the individual at the centre' (p. 23).

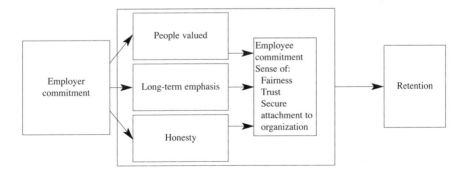

**Figure 7.3**  A partnership approach

Once this priority is established and communicated people will look for actions that also bear out the message. Valuing people is shown by treating them as a prized resource. Webber (1993) draws upon the ideas of Drucker (1992) and says it is 'the job of the organization to market itself to the knowledge worker. Managers, therefore, have to attract and motivate the best people; reward, recognize, and retain them; train, educate, and improve them – and, in the most remarkable reversal of all, serve and satisfy them' (p. 27). He builds his argument saying that it is the task of managers to ensure they remove any impediments to knowledge workers being productive.

Mathieu and Zajac (1990) report several practices which were strongly related to people's commitment and can be seen as signs that the organization values people. These practices were giving people job scope (correlation with commitment = 0.5) and getting leaders to be communicative (0.4), and participatory (0.4). Mathieu and Zajac also report that commitment was related to a lack of role conflict (0.3), role ambiguity (0.2) and role overload (0.2).

Meyer and Allen (1997) conclude their review of commitment by stressing the importance of work experiences that communicate the organization's support for its employees. They suggest that people must also be treated fairly and their sense of personal importance and competence needs to be enhanced by valuing the importance of their contributions.

The importance of valuing people is emphasized by Hope and Hope (1997). They concluded that 'surviving over many generations essentially means placing people rather than assets (and short-term profits) at the centre of strategy' (p. 43). This is backed up empirically by De Geus's (1997) study of what differentiates companies that survive from those that disappear. Studying 27 major companies that had survived over 100 years, the management of these companies had the overarching purpose to hand the company on to the next generation. He states 'A manager must let people grow within a community ... (and) ... must place commitment to people before assets ... and the perpetuation of the community before all other concerns' (p. 54). Indeed he notes that each of the companies changed their business portfolio at least once and that they were 'willing to scuttle assets in order to survive' (p. 55). The commitment to people was paramount.

## Emphasizing the long term

Almost by definition, gaining people's commitment and trust takes place over the long term and requires the organization to demonstrate its long-term commitment. Gratton (1997) describes how commitment at Hewlett-Packard took years to build and how the trust which is implicit in it will not be achieved if people are being asked to work in an environment of *ad hoc* initiatives. Similarly, Sennett (1998) declares 'chameleon institutions cannot command much loyalty'.

In order to behave consistently over the long term, treating people as a resource has to be part of the business strategy. It is a strategy based around winning in the market place by having a superior human resource. If the HR strategy is not integral to the business strategy, treating people as a resource is too easily compromised by day-to-day pressures. If that happens, trust will be destroyed. The strategy involves building a commitment that by its very nature takes time to establish but that can be undermined by isolated acts of 'betrayal'. Kinicki *et al.* (1992) showed that commitment was greater when people perceived the organization as committed to its HRM practices of commitment. They will be looking for the organization to behave consistently. They will also be looking for commitment to its people to be part of the organization's strategy to achieve prosperity.

Long-term consistency is especially important. Employment relationships are not like interpersonal relationships, where there comes a point that one has to, as Sorrentino *et al.* (1995) put it, set one's doubts aside and make a 'leap of faith'. In employment relationships this does not seem appropriate. People probably never quite leave the hypothesis-testing mode of establishing trust whereby any negative evidence will be noticed.

The strategy itself is the first way of showing a long-term commitment. However, people will look for deeds as well as words. At the level of deeds, the organization can adopt a variety of ways to emphasize long-term commitment. Pfeffer (1998) stresses the benefits from high commitment practices (especially promoting skill enhancement and giving control) and argues for the alignment of business strategy with HR management practices.

One particular way of building back a sense of commitment is the high-flyer scheme. Rajan and van Eupen (1997) have described how high-flyer programmes are being revived by a number of companies. Guest and Conway (1997) add that the practice of attempting to fill management vacancies with people from inside the organization is related to a positive psychological contract (covering fairness, trust and delivery of the deal). Conversely, if people from outside are brought in to fill senior positions, it can easily be taken as a sign of a lack of commitment to those people who are growing and developing within the organization.

However, by far the most telling deed that people will notice is not sticking by them. People will want to see that they are employable, not for the world in general but for their particular organization. There will be no trust if people feel the deal will be terminated by the organization if they no longer fully match its requirements. If this is the case, there is, in effect, no commitment of any worth. This makes it vital that people are chosen with the utmost care. Then, the organization must stand by all to whom the commitment was made, and not just discard people as if they were an item of fashion. If there is no sense of commitment to all then everyone is a potential loser and would be as well off moving as staying. Dismissing some people purely because they do not turn out to fit the vision perfectly is a message to all: the same might happen to them.

Yet, faced with the forces for change, there is a great temptation for organizations to behave in just this way and make people contingent. For example, Herriot and Anderson (1997) argue that 'work-role change is endemic, exponential in its effects' (p. 25) and that therefore 'selection needs to shift from being a one-off barrier to entry to being an on-going periodic re-appraisal of the fit between individual competencies and organisational, team and work-role demands' (p. 26). The risk of this is that it can easily lead organizations away from a long-term commitment and into treating everyone as fit only for the time being.

Apart from sticking by individuals, the long-term nature of the commitment will mean making some sacrifice of the present for the future if the organization itself is going through a difficult time. The idea of showing such a commitment is at the heart of Reichheld's approach. He observes that 'by showing people that the company won't stick by them in adversity, a firm can almost guarantee that the next time it's in trouble, its most talented employees will jump ship just when they're needed most' (p. 96). Supporting this, Guest and Conway (1997) found that having a stated policy of deliberately avoiding compulsory redundancies was related to a positive psychological contract.

Examples of organizations taking this approach in the UK are the John Lewis partnership and Proctor and Gamble. Donkin (1998a) reports that John Lewis retained 100 more staff than required in the last recession. The chairman – Stuart Hampson – is seeking the commitment of people and he sees this being brought about by their having 'spent time coming to know a company and its values' and by their identifying their personal future with that of the company. Proctor and Gamble follows a traditional approach to graduates, committing to them by having a policy of promotion from within, a policy that Donkin sees a 'a powerful selling point to graduates'. Donkin comments, 'employers who have abandoned the idea of mutual loyalty may wonder if there is any connection between P&G's attraction to graduates and its desire for them to have long-term careers with the company'.

## Behaving honestly

While the long-term commitment is vital, it must be an honest commitment. Organizations cannot guarantee jobs because they cannot guarantee the environment in which they operate. As John Stevens says in the preface to Kessler and Undy's (1996) report, inevitably, there will be times when 'organisations which have tried unsuccessfully with the full co-operation of their employees to make a success of a particular line of business may in the end have to decide reluctantly that "enough is enough" and closure may result' (p. vi).

This possibility needs to be recognized and dealt with honestly if it transpires. Hall and Mirvis (1995) also make it clear that 'most employers in the future will not be able to guarantee lifetime job security for even their core employees' (p. 343) and say it will be important for organizations to be 'honest with people about business conditions and assist them with outplacement' (p. 342). Trust and honesty are, indeed, integral to each other. Green (1998) illustrates how the core can be treated with honesty. He describes how at Forward Trust they 'admitted to the workforce that we had misled them in the past' (p. 44). He also stresses that they should be treated as adults and as problem solvers if things go wrong for the company. Thus he describes how part of the company was 'virtually wiped out' by government legislation and how the company went into detailed discussions with staff about their futures. The result was that most people were redeployed and of the 10 per cent of redundancies some were voluntary and some inevitable because of people not wanting to relocate. He comments, 'in the past, we would have decided who was going and told them' (p. 45).

Coulson-Thomas (1997) sums it up by saying, 'The emphasis should be upon openness, loyalty, trust, variety, tolerance and debate, the very areas that are often undermined by corporate change programmes' (p. 33).

## FORMING A PARTNERSHIP

The notion of honesty as well as valuing people and making a long-term commitment conveys the idea of entering into a partnership with them. People are treated as stakeholders. This can be related to Rousseau and Wade-Benzoni's (1995) division of contracts into short- and long-term with performance either 'specified' or 'not specified'. Organizations have tended to move to the short-term contracts with performance specified. In order to show a commitment, they need to move in the opposite direction. They certainly must move to the long term; arguably, they also need to move to the 'not specified', because the future cannot be specified. Long-term and not specified contracts are called 'relational' by Rousseau and Wade-Benzoni and are analogous to a family business. In such contracts, there are high levels of commitment, both affective and continuance.

Hall and Mirvis (1995) also subscribe to a variant of the partnership approach. They say that 'some employees might be treated like "partners" with a share in ownership' (p. 342). Reichheld advocates such an approach, suggesting what comes near to either a legal partnership or a franchise which he describes as 'value-sharing' (p. 287). He says that, in the case of employees, partnership produces among other benefits those of alignment, flexibility and talent. By alignment, he means staff are aligned with the organization. He gives the example of the agents at State Farm Insurance. They receive a gross commission and hence are aligned to the company in the need to contain costs. Flexibility comes from partners being in a network rather than a large bureaucratic organization. Finally talented people will be attracted by the opportunity to be partners and to be rewarded for their performance, an opportunity that is lacking with Fortune 500 corporations, he says.

Clearly, there are lessons from Reichheld's words and these ought to be considered in implementing a strategy of partnership. However, his approach clearly does not meet the needs of larger publicly owned companies, which, by definition, could not make their staff legal partners. It seems worth exploring whether some form of the partnership approach could be made to apply to most companies. If it is to do so, partnership needs to be recast as an attitude rather than a legal agreement. For the organization to offer partnership, it needs an attitude of commitment, of being in the relationship for the long term. It is also an attitude of standing by the members of staff and of helping them through difficulties and times when they need to change.

It is such an attitude of partnership to which Hirsh and Jackson (1996) seem to be referring when they contrast it with the 'over to you' approach. Hirsh and Jackson describe how the organizations in their survey of 15 major UK-based employers (including BP and BT) had moved back from such an approach to having a partnership. The reason is the 'concern about how to retain and motivate highly skilled employees who are being told to look after themselves' (p. 21). Other evidence comes from Prickett (1998d), who reports a survey that showed that organizations saw that a 'happier partnership' was more likely to retain people than pay. Jackson (1998c) also discusses how a partnership model is the direction towards which more sophisticated companies are leaning. A sign that organizations might be making these changes is the focusing of selection procedures on person–organization fit (Anderson and Ostroff, 1997). People join the organization. They are not selected for a job or role. In line with this, Hamel and Prahalad (1994) describe the need for people with 'a deep sense of community' (p. 320). This need not mean that everyone is the same in the organization, any more than everyone is the same in a sports club. They are, however, united by some common interest and common values.

## MEETING PEOPLE'S NEEDS

Showing commitment, gaining trust and offering partnership are all very well. People also need to pay their bills. As Altman and Post (1996) remind us, the employment relationship starts off as a transaction. People will only join an organization if it helps them meet their needs, and they cannot be expected to stay if their needs cease to be met. They need the transactions of continuance commitment in addition to the commitment of affective commitment.

The literature on interpersonal commitment suggests that meeting people's needs is a precursor to gaining their commitment. As described by Agnew *et al.* (1998), interpersonal commitment emerges out of dependence which, in turn, rests on 'the degree that a relationship provides good outcomes and to the degree that the outcomes available in alternative relationships are poor' (p. 940). If applied to organizations, this draws neatly our attention to the problems they face. Under the 'dependence model', organizations must ensure that they provide good outcomes, and this is against a backdrop of alternative employment always being available for good people.

The 'dependence model' is extended by taking into account the amount that each side has already invested in the relationship. The 'investment model' suggests that organizations need to encourage people to invest in the relationship. Presumably, people will only make this investment if they perceive the reward to risk ratio as suitable.

## SUMMARY

To win a talent war, talented people must be retained. The policy of making people contingent has created careerists, people who are avoidant in terms of organizational attachment. The policy has fuelled the talent war and clearly cannot work to win it. If people feel they could be 'let go' at any moment, they will be best advised moving to another organization which offers the same or a better transaction with a greater prospect of the transaction being ongoing. They are better off going to an organization that offers a relational contract. Such a contract involves the organization showing people commitment. It shows commitment to gain commitment.

This means valuing people, having a long-term perspective and behaving honestly. It means striking up an attitude of partnership. Clearly, it might not be possible to offer this to everyone. Those to whom it is offered need to form a clearly segregated core.

The commitment and trust that will be fostered enable people to build on an organizational attachment style based on security. The style will help people cope with change, rather than them having the resistant and defensive style of the anxious-ambivalent person or the pure self-reliance of people who are avoidant. Coping with change will reinforce and bear out the organization's commitment to them. The same virtuous circle is set up with respect to learning. Commitment breeds trust which enables learning which renews the desire by the organization to offer commitment.

The strategy to build and retain the winning resource of talented people needs to be part of the business strategy. Otherwise, it will be all too easy for expediency to set in and for people in the core to be treated as a cost.

## HAS THE HORSE BOLTED?

It might all be too late. The reward to risk ratio that governs whether people will invest in a relationship with the organization might have been altered by the rewards becoming less attractive and the risks too great. Having given the core a mixed message, able people have learnt to live independently. They have learnt that organizations will always need them. In addition, maybe, the emphasis on portability and mobility has become endemic so that people feel they have failed if they are not in the transfer market, flattered by the head-hunter's call. They have become avoidant. They are careerists.

While there is plenty of evidence that people have become independent, there is also evidence and reason to believe that people still would like a degree of commitment from and to an organization. In the UK, Kessler and Undy (1996) report the majority of employees still 'looked for job security and career development with their existing employer' (p. 21). In addition, Maitland (1998a) reports on research by Jane Sturges that suggested that 'most graduates expect a long-term career with their company'. Sturges is quoted as saying they are also 'very committed to the companies they're going to work with'.

In other words, it is possible that people would still like a deal which will exchange commitment between themselves and their employer, albeit not a deal of paternalism. It must be a meeting of equal partners. The reason to believe that people might be retained by the offer of trust and commitment stems from a belief that people will want to form a commitment to an organization as long as that commitment does not appear foolish and in bad faith. None the less, the idea that it is all too late is but one of many siren voices to tempt organizations back to transactional contracts.

# Siren voices to short-termism      8

Having a long-term strategy to build and retain talent can easily meet with objections. There is, indeed, a catalogue of excuses for getting back to treating people as a cost. These doubts can readily lead organizations back to creating mixed messages about commitment. Nine of these siren voices will be considered.

## 1. HUMAN CAPITAL IS NOT CENTRAL TO SUCCESS

There might be some organizations which depend more on brawn than brain. Others depend largely on equipment. However, it is hard to conceive of an organization of any size that does not need to build and retain some core of talented people who, among other functions, will be the repository of the organization's knowledge, the retainers of customers and the strategists for the future.

## 2. WE ARE NOT THE RETAINING TYPE

Miles and Snow (1978) drew the distinction between four strategic missions. They are:

- **Prospectors** These are organizations that thrive on product innovation and creating new markets
- **Defenders** Firms with a narrow product or market base
- **Analysers** They deliver newer products and services, without the innovativeness of prospectors
- **Reactors** They are buffeted by their environment

They say that prospectors will tend to select on the basis of expertise and recruit externally. Defenders will emphasize developing people from within. Analysers will also place an emphasis on loyalty. Finally reactors are clearly more concerned with retrenchment than building a core. On the face of it, building a core seems to apply more to defenders and analysers than to prospectors and reactors.

Miles and Snow's work was drawn upon a decade later by Sonnenfeld and Peiperl (1988). They describe two main aspects to career systems. The first is whether the organization brings people in from the external labour market to fill vacancies or relies on the internal supply of people. The second is whether people are moved across assignments on the basis of being a 'star performer' or by being a 'solid contributor'. They use these two dimensions to build a two-by-two model of career systems. They suggest that the resulting four possibilities are each suited to particular industries. For example, they place many professional service organizations within the quadrant that relies upon external supply and star performers. They label this the 'baseball team' quadrant. In contrast, manufacturing organizations are placed within 'academies' which aim to develop star performers from within. Public sector agencies are seen as 'clubs', interested in retaining solid performers. Finally, retailers and organizations in natural resources are 'fortresses'. They are on the wane, engaged in retrenchment.

Sonnenfeld and Peiperl suggest that policies for long-term retention will tend to be found more in clubs and academies than in the other two types. Moreover these two types of organization will also attract people looking for advancement and security. In contrast, baseball teams will attract people who identify more with their profession than the organization. The overall model is summarized in Table 8.1, which also shows (in italics) the correspondence with Miles and Snow's ideas.

On the face of it, a strategy for winning the talent war by commitment applies only to 'clubs' and 'academies'. However, one might question whether the exclusion of fortresses (reactors) and baseball teams (prospectors) from the strategy is appropriate today. First, fortresses might be in the position they are in because they lack a competent core. Second, the baseball team model might be naive in imagining they can hire externally just because they want to and in assuming people's retention is not a

**Table 8.1**

|                 | Solid performer                        | Star performer                          |
| --------------- | -------------------------------------- | --------------------------------------- |
| External supply | Fortress–retrenchment<br>*Reactors*    | Baseball team–recruitment<br>*Prospectors* |
| Internal supply | Club–retention<br>*Defenders*          | Academy–development<br>*Analysers*      |

priority. People might not be available when they are wanted and the people who leave will leave when it suits them, perhaps when they can command the highest transfer fee. These organizations might be better advised building a core of adaptable people, treating them in a way that will both retain them and be appropriate for managing knowledge workers today. People are generally more likely to give a star performance if they are shown commitment and have trust in the organization.

## 3.   WE WILL GIVE THEM GOBS OF MONEY (AND SACK THEM IF THEY FAIL)

Organizations might be tempted to follow the image of the finance sector of Wall Street and the City of London and secure their knowledge workers by money. The approach is patently short-term. If money is all that is on offer to people, there is actually little hold on people. Evidence of this comes almost daily in reports in the *Wall Street Journal* and *Financial Times*. Indeed, whole teams are poached on a regular basis. For example, the *Financial Times* (17 March 1999) carried the item that 'Lehman Brothers has raided Deutsche Bank's UK mergers and acquisitions department again, announcing the recruitment of "an experienced team" of eight more bankers'. No doubt Deutsche Bank is profitable. The imponderable is how much more successful they might be with a strategy that retained people through engaging their commitment. Of course, people would still need to be paid the market rate. The objective would be to match competitors on salary and trump them on strategy.

The tactic of using a mix of pay and punishment is discussed by Williams and Dobson (1997). They draw attention to the division of companies into 'financial control companies' and 'strategic planning companies'. The former, exemplified by Hanson Trust, place all their emphasis on short-term profit performance, rewarding people who meet their targets and replacing those who do not. It can be assumed that financial control companies will only be successful in the long term if they can readily obtain people at short notice who will yield high performance.

The assumption that human capital can satisfactorily be bought in a 'just-in-time' fashion seems the foundation of the headhunter's trade. It is the attitude of 'crossing the bridge when we come to it'. The problem is that people of the right talent might not be available to be hired in when the time comes that they are needed. Gratton (1997) gives the example the current difficulties facing firms in China, where she says the great difficulty is to 'attract, recruit and retain management talent' (p. 24). In China, people simply cannot be bought in from the external labour market. She goes on to describe how Motorola anticipated this impossibility and took steps to ensure they had a long-term strategy to provide for their future management and leadership. What applies to China in a stark form applies elsewhere, albeit perhaps less graphically.

Even if talented people are available, they need to be prepared and socialized. Williams and Dobson (1997) illustrate this using the examples of organizations such as the armed forces, police, clearing banks, airlines. They have to invest a great deal in training because, 'trained army officers, police, bank managers or pilots do not normally exist in the labour market' (p. 231). The unavailability of such people leads to an emphasis on retention through rewards and career management. The types of organization in the examples of Williams and Dobson use a form of socialization that is labelled as 'divestiture' by van Maanen and Schein (1979). It involves building or rebuilding the person and applies not just to overtly uniformed organizations like Disneyworld and McDonald's but also to the ranks of white-shirted managers at many major corporations.

In contrast to those that need divestiture, van Maanen and Schein (1979) point out that the organization might be able to take on people who are semi-socialized having worked in the same line of business. However, there will still be a period of moulding for these people. Van Maanen and Schein label this tactic investiture. As an example it would apply to taking on a trained lawyer.

Even if investiture applies, the approach of buying in talent does not sit entirely happily with the modern form of organization, after the transition from rigid bureaucracies to lean, flat and dynamic bodies. People are no longer mere position holders. A new person cannot simply arrive, read the files and get to work. They need to build a network and make use of a wealth of knowledge that can only build up over time. The higher up the organization one goes, the truer it becomes that people cannot simply be 'parachuted in' to key posts. They need to go through a lengthy socialization process or risk being rejected by the culture of the organization. This is a very clear implication of van Maanen and Schein's model of socialization which presents roles in organizations as defined by function, hierarchy and inclusion. Inclusion involves movement 'toward the "center of things"' (p. 221). They comment that 'newcomers to most hierarchical levels and functional areas in virtually all organizations inevitably remain "on the edge" of organizational affairs for some time after entrance for a host of reasons' (p. 222). For example, people are tested formally or informally before they are given access to organizational secrets and they need to learn the unofficial norms that operate. All this takes time.

The analysis helps explain why it is risky to try to bring in outsiders to senior roles. Jackson (1998a), reporting from the World Economic Forum at Davos, says that CEOs of large corporates were in agreement that CEOs should be appointed from inside the organization, if at all possible. The reason is simply the differences in cultures between companies. Jackson quotes Percy Barnevik, chairman of ABB, who said 'the idea that a professional chief executive can run anything is plain wrong'. Barnevik went on to illustrate this by saying the person who runs Nestlé will not be the right person for his company.

Examples to support this argument present themselves on pretty much a daily basis. For example Donkin (1997b) described how the following companies had all lost externally appointed CEOs shortly before he wrote his article:

- **Taylor Woodrow**  A large UK property and construction group. The CEO resigned after six months in post. He was the first CEO from outside the group and Donkin comments that 'his style did not match that of his fellow directors'

- **WH Smith**  CEO resigned after 18 months leaving the company vulnerable to take-over

- **AT&T**  An externally recruited successor-designate to the CEO was, after nine months, told he would not be getting the top job. His pay and compensation amounted to $26million

Donkin (1997b) adds National Freight Corporation, Glaxo Wellcome and Waste Management to the list of companies with failed CEO appointments. He observes that 'companies that groom successors not only save on the recruitment costs of an outside search but also avoid the risk of an appointment turning sour' (p. 16). Pfeffer (1994) adds to this conclusion, saying how 'there are numerous tales of firms managed by those with little understanding of the basic operations, often with miserable results' (p. 53).

## 4.  ANYWAY, WE ARE LEAVING

There are many small businesses for which developing and retaining high-flyers might seem someone else's problem. The owner/leader plans to sell the business on to someone else who will be the leader. Of course, the prospective new buyer will be well advised to audit the intellectual capital, but the shaky psychological contract with people who have been 'sweated' to produce good financial returns might be hidden from view.

The line of thinking that applies to the departing small business proprietor nowadays applies to many large organizations. They have mimicked small businesses. They have reorganized and devolved all responsibilities to their lines of business. These lines of business might see themselves as inherently less permanent than the group to which they belong. They and their management will have a relatively short-term perspective and perhaps be less concerned than the corporation about growing their future leadership. Like the small business owner who hopes to hand on the problems to the next person, these heads of lines of business will be more focused on the short-term financial figures than on growing and retaining a talented resource. Expediency becomes the order of the day and there is a powerful force to treat people as a cost rather than a resource.

This 'selfish' line of thinking runs the risk for the small businessperson of having a less valuable business to sell if key staff have left. For the large devolved corporation, it spells problems for the future. There are two ways of avoiding them. One is to urge that those charged with the long-term interests of the organization insist that the lines of business take on the long-term view. In particular, it is up to the boards of companies to question managers about whether the future leadership is being installed. The better CEO and board, particularly the chairperson and non-executive directors, will look to the company's long-term future. They will need to ensure that heads of lines of business are accountable for implementing the strategy for retaining talent. The second way forward is for heads of lines of business to recognize that the short-term savings from treating people as a cost might well be less than the short-term benefits from treating them as a resource. These benefits are in the form of being able to retain people for their immediate contribution. Once people start walking out of the door in sufficient numbers, this logic will become insistent.

## 5.   PEOPLE WILL LEAVE ANYWAY

Pfeffer (1994) declares that if the organization makes a commitment, 'norms of reciprocity tend to guarantee that this commitment is repaid' (p. 31). This might invoke a hollow laugh from anyone who has felt committed to staff, but has received their letters of resignation. None the less, the response to the feeling of let-down is not to give up. Clearly, people will leave. The rationale for the strategy is that more will leave without it than with it.

## 6.   WE ARE BIG AND WELL-KNOWN

Of course, organizations that are household names will find the interest of potential applicants easier to engage than will unknown organizations. Nevertheless, being well known does not give a right to attract or retain people. The fact is that there will be other well-known organizations that will offer not just their name but also to treat people as a resource. The best people will migrate to the best organizations. It is only by retaining the best people that organizations will retain their name.

## 7. NEED FOR FRESH BLOOD

It is perfectly reasonable to argue that some turnover is healthy. It brings fresh blood. For example, Robinson and Miner (1996) discuss the notion that a 'modest level of turnover' can be beneficial by augmenting the collective knowledge of an organization. Hamel and Prahalad (1994) discuss hiring outsiders as a way of changing the way an organization thinks. They use the analogy of genetics talking about outsiders cross-breeding and altering the organization's genetic code. However, as they say, this is a slow way to bring about change. Furthermore, it is one thing to make the best of some level of turnover; it is another to encourage it. Such a policy goes completely against the notion of building and retaining a resource. Donkin (1998a) reports how Proctor and Gamble counter the fresh blood argument by saying that 'if you place a strong emphasis on career development, constantly providing new challenges for staff, then the existing blood will be as fresh as any available from outside'.

Whatever strategy is followed to retain people, some turnover will obviously remain. The need deliberately to encourage turnover in order to introduce fresh blood does not seem particularly convincing with respect to people below senior management. However, at senior levels and particularly at the CEO level, the decision might be taken to introduce fresh blood to bring about major change. Apart from the socialization problems referred to when discussing buying people in, the added difficulty, as Hunt (1999b) points out, is that the new CEO often comes with a group of trusted lieutenants. This will not be greeted with equanimity by those within the organization, particularly if they had thought they were being grown with a management development programme. Hunt suggests that 'once a board starts searching for managers outside, it is predictable that some of its best people will soon start to look elsewhere for promotion. It is always the high-flyers who depart first, leaving a layer of less impressive colleagues.' Bringing in fresh blood at the top risks being self-defeating and creating a self-perpetuating lack of internal talent. It seems to stand only to benefit the revenue stream of headhunting firms.

## 8.  WE NEED REFRESHED BLOOD

A related argument is the need for refreshed blood. There clearly are careers for which it is helpful for people to work in different sectors. The manager does a spell as a consultant or vice versa. The gamekeeper tries a spell of poaching. This argument is nowadays regularly applied to the public sector, whose staff are advised to spend some time in the private sector. It is a theme developed by Mirvis and Hall (1996b) who speculate that people will move from the core into 'a job in a supplier company or consulting firm, working as an individual contractor on selected projects, and then returning to the fold as a senior core contributor' (p. 82). Clearly, this type of career move is not uncommon and in some occupations it can benefit both the employer and the member of staff. However, recognizing that people will move in this way is different from celebrating it. The problem is that with the person who leaves both knowledge and invest-ment are lost. There is no guarantee at all that an equivalent replacement will be found and, even in the best-case scenario, getting back to normal will involve a cost of recruitment and socialization. It is self-evidently expensive and organizations need to consider carefully whether the bene-fits outweigh the costs. A better way forward might be a system of long-term secondments by which people gain the valuable experience without being lost to their organization.

## 9.  WE CANNOT AFFORD TO IMPLEMENT THIS STRATEGIC APPROACH

It might sound trite, but the retort is that you cannot afford not to. The practices that treat people as a resource have been shown convincingly to impact the bottom line. Huselid (1995) examined the relationship between 'high performance work practices' and turnover, productivity and corpo-rate financial performance. High performance work practices were in two categories. The first was labelled 'employee skills and organizational structure'. They covered practices that were meant to enhance the knowl-edge, skills and abilities of employees and to help them put these attributes to good use in performing their roles. Huselid labelled the second category, 'employee motivation' and it covered such issues as performance appraisal, performance-related pay and promotion on merit.

He found both categories of work practices were related to turnover and productivity, and the bottom line was that 'each one standard deviation increase in High Performance Work Practices increased cash flow $3814' (p. 659) per employee. In an earlier report on (presumably) the same data,

Huselid (1994) reports that an 'average expected annual increase in profits' (p. 85) of $7868 per employee would come from the same degree of improvement in the practices.

In support of these results, Prickett (1998a) describes how a US-wide Gallup survey demonstrated that businesses with staff who feel valued and who have scope for development 'enjoy up to 27 per cent higher profits and 22 per cent higher productivity than average'. In the UK, research by Patterson, *et al.* (1997) suggests similar conclusions. They looked at employees' satisfaction with a range of aspects of work, including fellow team members, immediate boss, the way the firm is managed, hours of work, job security and chances of promotion and attention paid to suggestions. They found that satisfaction as measured by these and the other indicators accounted for 16 per cent of the variation in subsequent changes in productivity and 5 per cent of the variation in subsequent changes in profitability. These results were after controlling for prior productivity and profitability.

Going into greater detail, they borrowed Quinn and Rohrbaugh's (1981) models of organizational culture. Quinn and Rohrbaugh put forward four competing models of how an organization should operate as follows:

- **Human relations**   The emphasis is on norms and values associated with belonging, trust and participation. People's motivation comes from attachment, cohesiveness and group membership

- **Open systems**   The emphasis is on change and innovation. Motivation is from growth, variety and stimulation

- **Rational goal**   The emphasis is on the pursuit and attainment of well-defined objectives. Motivation is from competition and achievement

- **Internal process**   The emphasis is on stability, internal organization and adherence to rules. Motivation is from security, order and rules and regulations

Patterson *et al.* measured each organization on the extent to which it operated according to each of the four models. They related differences in terms of each of the four to variations in profitability and productivity. They found that differences between organizations in terms of the internal process and open systems models bore little relationship to variation in profit or productivity. On the other hand differences between organizations in terms of the rational goal and human resources models were related to variations in productivity. The result was particularly striking for the human relations model. Twenty-nine per cent of variation between organizations in their productivity was predicted by differences in the levels of concern for employee welfare, autonomy, supervisory support and training. Further, the differences in terms of human relations was the only one of the four models to predict change in company profitability.

It appears from this research that organizations are both more profitable and more productive by following the basic approach of the strategy. As a reminder, they emphasize the norms and values associated with belonging, trust and participation. People's motivation comes from attachment, cohesiveness and group membership.

## CONCLUSION

Clearly, it would be foolish entirely to dismiss every siren voice. However, many do not bear close scrutiny. Organizations that want to be star performers will want to have staff who are star performers. This can only be achieved by implementing a strategy to attract, develop, motivate and retain those staff.

Part Two suggests how to put the strategy into practice. In this we are helped by Reichheld's (1996) observation that 'loyalty is not only philosophy and strategy; it speaks also to operations, because it offers a set of practical measures for implementing strategy' (p. 302). When considering each of the practical issues such as recruitment and development, we can be guided by the principle of gaining commitment by showing commitment, trust and honesty.

# Part Two

# Implementing the strategy of gaining commitment by showing commitment

# Who are you calling core? 9

The heart of the strategy to win the talent war is to secure people's commitment by offering them a relational contract as well as meeting their transactional needs. These people make up the core. The starting point of implementing the strategy for the core is deciding who makes up this group. The answer is provided by considering two factors. First, the size and make-up of the group of people from whom the organization would like to have a commitment. Second, the number to whom a commitment can be made with the realistic and honest prospect of it being honoured. Comparing the two might well present a dilemma. The organization might like to include more people in the core than it is able to make a commitment towards. This dilemma needs to be confronted and resolved. Otherwise, the organization will be tempted to fudge the situation and tell all those from whom it wants a commitment that they are core without being able to honour the commitment in return. In due course, when tested, the organization's commitment to the core will be shown to be empty. The core will see that its members are treated with what amounts to the same attitude as the periphery. Being in the core will cease having any meaning and trust will be destroyed.

Resolving the dilemma can be achieved by scaling down the number the organization puts in the core. It can also be resolved by scaling up the overall price the organization is prepared to pay for having a core in terms of making commitments it will honour. However, the organization cannot simply write a blank cheque in terms of its commitments. People will see it for what it is, namely an empty promise. How the organization resolves the discrepancy will be influenced by its forecast of the future. Almost by definition, the further into the future the focus is, the vaguer the picture will become and so the organization will need to be more circumspect in terms of making commitments to its staff. This might lead responsible organizations to keep the core tight. The commitment is not gilt-edged. Clearly, there will be unforeseen events that will cause the most committed organization to have to shed people even from a tightly defined core in order to survive. This was the case for oil companies at the start of 1999 as the price of crude sank below $10 a barrel. Their difficulties could not reasonably have been foreseen. However, this is very different from an organization that expands its 'core' on the upwave, knowing that it has no commitment in the downwave. The core become, in effect, casual workers. For example, many companies in the finance industry are known for a policy of hiring people in bull markets and shedding them when conditions become less profitable. The people who are hired and then fired cannot possibly be considered part of the core. There is no real commitment to them. If the organization fails to draw a line between these 'seasonal' workers and others, everyone will regard themselves as subject to the same contingent contract. They would be foolish staying if a better transaction is offered by a competitor and their organization will suffer the consequences in terms of turnover. This seems to be precisely what happens in many City of London and Wall Street firms. People know their employers have little commitment to them and move singly or in teams when a better deal is on offer.

While many organizations restrict the number in the core to whom a commitment is offered, some organizations have defined the way forward as being to make everyone core. Green (1998) describes how, at Forward Trust, they have done away with the distinction, seeing it as 'misplaced'. Everyone is core. The trick with this is to ensure that it is more than rhetoric and 'spin'. Everyone should only be core if there is a genuine commitment to them. Otherwise, everyone is periphery.

Never the less, the more widespread commitment by Forward Trust is one that an increasing number of organizations appear to be deciding they need to make. Holbeche (1998) says, 'increasingly, succession planning activities in some sectors are being extended beyond a small privileged group of "key employees" to include a much wider group. The question being asked in such organizations is "who is key?" in this era of knowledge workers and intellectual capital' (p. 74). She suggests that this question is quite obviously pertinent in industries like IT which are highly knowledge or skill based and reports how Sun Microsystems UK have a system for the top 80 per cent alongside a conventional high-flyer development programme.

The widening of the number included in the core seems to be precisely to gain their commitment by offering a commitment. These organizations want to include more of their knowledge workers in the core to retain their services. In order to do so they need to offer a genuine commitment to these people.

However, not every organization can simply declare all its intellectual capital, its knowledge workers, to be core, without any further adjustments to its structure. One has only to look at the major accountancy firms that take on hundreds of graduates. These people clearly do not all have a future within their organizations. There cannot be a long-term commitment to these people. They are mainly on a time-limited transaction. Training in exchange for audit work.

If such organizations find that turnover is too high or too rapid among these limited-term staff, they will have to examine how they can widen the number to whom they make a commitment. The organization will have to examine how work is divided between people and it will have to choose people who are content to work in a flat structure.

In summary, organizations have to decide the size of the core group to whom they can offer a commitment. However, it would make no sense at all if the core did not at least include the present leaders and potential future leaders of the organization. These people are the key talent on whom the strategy is focused. The organization must make a commitment to the high-potential group of people who are seen as being on track for leadership positions. It must also honour its commitment to the plateaued pool, people who no longer are seen as having high potential, but to whom the organization made a commitment as core staff.

The core might well also include as many other talented people as possible because the organization wants to retain them for qualities other than leadership competencies. For example, pilots might be part of the core of an airline but they do not all possess leadership talent. Likewise a software consultancy might include in its core analysts and programmers who need to be retained for their professional skills.

## THE HIGH-POTENTIAL GROUP

Almost by definition, the group of future leaders needs to be relatively constrained in number. It needs to reflect the number of leadership positions to be 'inherited'. People will be selected into it because they have the attributes that will enable them to become leaders. The people within the high-potential group need to be reviewed and those who remain need a particular focus on their development. Some of these people will not realize their potential and for others what is required in the future may not be what was anticipated when they were selected. They will join the plateaued pool.

It certainly seems wise for organizations to concentrate on a small number of people in the high-potential group, if only because there is only a small number of positions to cater for. This is the approach of BP. Holbeche (1998) describes the company as focusing upon people with potential for the top 80 posts. The individuals who join the high-potential programme are assigned to 'cohorts' based on their stage of leadership development. The *IPD guide on international management development* (1997) describes Standard Chartered Bank as another company that places strict limits to its high-potential group. It has established a 'Global Talent Bank'. This is made up of some 150 managers across the group's businesses who have been identified as high-flyers who are candidates for key jobs and whose development is actively monitored.

These examples make clear that some organizations keep the number in the high-potential group very small indeed. They include only the number needed to replace the leadership of the organization. Keeping the group restricted in this way means that the people in it stand a realistic chance of realizing their ambitions of advancement. As such, it implements the strategy by offering talented people the transaction they want as well as the relationship.

Perhaps because of these considerations, Pritchard (1996) describes how UK banks, including NatWest and Midland (part of HSBC Group) are recruiting a smaller number of better graduates than in the past when they took on more than could be developed into senior managers. Rajan and van Eupen (1997) and Pickard (1997b) give more detail on the example of NatWest. The bank has a 'next generation' group of some 250 high-potential managers, some of whom will join the highly select group with potential to become the future leadership. They are generally in their mid-30s and being in the group gives these relatively young people the sense that they do not have to serve time before they can advance. As a further example, Pucik (1998) describes how Asea and Brown Boveri (ABB) has a core of 500 global managers out of its 200 000 workforce. Restricting the number in the high-potential group in the manner of NatWest and ABB again avoids making commitments that cannot be honoured. In particular, it means that these organizations avoid having a lot of frustrated individuals who would like to advance but who are unable to do so in the contemporary flat structure of organizations. Without the restriction in number, there is the danger of losing the faith of people who will feel they have been deceived by the possibility of advancement that could never have been delivered.

## THE BOUNDARY TO THE HIGH-POTENTIAL GROUP

Movement into the high-potential group needs to be carefully controlled. To identify people for the group and select them for fast-track development, the organization might use an assessment centre that focuses on the competencies required for leadership. An example is Tarmac Professional Services (Woodruffe, 1997) that used an assessment centre to choose a select group of people for an accelerated management development programme. Some organizations also use 360 degree feedback processes to identify talent as well as for individual development (Bracken *et al.*, 1997).

The advantage of the assessment centre is that it offers the chance for an objective review of people's competencies. Deciding who will be seen at the centre will normally be based on the recommendations of line managers. However, some organizations include the possibility of self-nomination to overcome any problems raised by people feeling they have not been given the chance to show their potential.

Obviously, there will be plenty of organizations that rely entirely on the recommendations of line managers to identify potential. Whether or not an assessment centre is added, the 'buy in' of the line to the process is crucial, as their support will be vital when people come to implement their development plans.

## THE PLATEAUED POOL

Hirsh and Jackson (1996) comment that 'fast-tracks' need to concentrate less on 'crown princes' and more on developing all the people who are within the high potential group. These people only remain in the group 'for as long as they continue to show unusual ability' (p. 22). The major test of the organization's commitment is what happens if people no longer show this potential. It is essential that the organization honours its commitment to them as core staff. Otherwise, everyone in the high potential group will see themselves as candidates for the 'no potential' group of people who are 'let go'. Being in the core becomes a devalued currency.

The organization therefore has to manage a pool of plateaued people. Some of its members might choose to leave, but they certainly should not feel they have been thrown out. They need to be dealt with in an honest manner and counselled about their future prospects. Those who want to make a continued contribution to the organization must be seen by their colleagues to be treated fairly.

## THE TALENT POOL

The particular emphasis of this book is the group seen as the future leadership of the organization. However, as already noted, there will be a larger or smaller group of other talented individuals who the organization will place in the core because it wants to retain them by offering them a commitment. By definition, the people in this talent pool should be there for reasons other than their leadership abilities and the promise made to them should be other than that they will advance to be leaders. If this is not made clear at the outset, the organization risks forming a core of people who cannot hope to realize their ambitions and who possess qualities that do not fully match the organization's requirements. The outset must mean the time that people are recruited. Being less than honest in order to fill vacancies risks creating hostages to fortune that will destroy a strategy based on trust and good faith.

# Roll up for the mystery tour: recruiting the talent army   10

## SPIN OR SUBSTANCE

Ghoshal and Bartlett (1998) emphasize the importance of recruitment to gaining competitive advantage. Talent is in short supply. The ability to recruit talented people is the obvious first step to winning the talent war. Jackson (1998b) states the issue well. He says, 'The biggest single headache for professional service firms, senior partners will unanimously tell you, is attracting enough bright young people.' He describes the two limiting factors as competition from other employers and demographics, with the number of under-25s in the UK population dropping 14 per cent since 1971. Prickett (1998d) also gives testimony on the difficulties that recruiters face, reporting that in the UK 'the number of companies having difficulties filling their graduate vacancies has increased every year since 1993'.

In the light of these problems, it is tempting to try to attract people with empty promises and to make rushed choices. This is a road that seems destined to lead to a name as a bad employer, serving only to make future recruitment even more difficult. Instead, the need is to get organized, be attractive, tell the truth and make well-considered decisions.

## GETTING ORGANIZED

Ghoshal and Bartlett (1998) make clear that recruitment requires consistent focused effort. As an example, they describe how Microsoft has a process for bringing in 400 graduates each year. The company makes sure that candidates are 'interviewed by at least three – and sometimes up to 10 – "microsoftees"'. Even more strikingly, the company maintains a team of 200 people who are responsible for recruiting a further 2000 people each year. They target 'the best and the brightest people' already working in the industry. The approach is painstaking. Recruiters keep open lines of communication with people who are identified as targets on the basis that one day they will feel like leaving their current employer.

The same focused and painstaking approach is applied by Proctor and Gamble in their graduate recruitment. Donkin (1998a) reports that the company sends its graduate trainees to visit universities because they know who to approach and can give a first-hand account to potential recruits of what the work is like. He also reports that P&G have internships in the summer vacation before the students' final year at university and that people who have been on internships make up half the graduate intake.

The targeting of potential graduate entrants is taken a step further by some employers who use headhunters to approach potential applicants. This practice is discussed by Arkin (1999) who describes how university tutors give headhunters the names of high-flyers and how being approached in this way is flattering and yields a recruitment advantage to the organizations who do it.

Prickett (1998d) reports another tactic being adopted, which is to get people signed up early. This, for example, is said to be IBM's approach. The company interviews in the autumn for people to join the following summer. This is intended to enable them to get the best recruits before their competitors.

All these examples illustrate that recruiting talented people needs to be well thought out and involves a campaign to which time and resources are allocated. As much as anything, the effort shows to potential recruits how important they are and how the organization sees them as part of a strategy for its future.

## Looking in the right places

Part of getting organized is knowing where to look for talented people. In seeking graduates, organizations are faced with a bewildering array of educational institutions and feel they have to target particular institutions and departments. In choosing targets, a winning answer is to look in the less obvious places and overcome the obvious temptation to confine one's efforts to good departments of 'better' universities. As Arkin (1999) says, those who so confine themselves 'could be making a rod for their own backs' (p. 43), as they will be competing with all the other employers also looking in the obvious places. A sophisticated selection procedure should enable a more adventurous organization to identify talent elsewhere and away from the competition of every other employer.

The herd instinct also applies when seeking senior-level people. Companies frequently use the same hit list of targets. Donkin (1998c) reports a headhunter who names GE, Motorola and Pepsi as the favourites, but, of course these companies have not got a limitless supply of people waiting to be tempted away from them. Indeed it is a contradiction in terms to expect people to be so tempted. If these companies are so great, people will want to stay. Again, a sophisticated selection procedure should help identify talent in less obvious places.

## Widening the net

Apart from looking more widely in terms of places, the organization will need to look more widely in terms of people. It should be seeking talent in terms of competencies and not clones in terms of background. If the organization has concluded it needs to recruit greater diversity, it needs to make itself attractive to such people, quite apart from protecting them once they have joined. To make itself attractive, perhaps it needs to present itself as welcoming of differences and not rigidly defined in terms of its organizational personality. The more rigid the definition, the more it will restrict itself to people 'like us'. It therefore needs to present images in its recruitment literature of diverse people who have been successful employees. It also needs to take great care in its selection procedures not to recruit within a particular mould. The interview is particularly prone to this tendency and interviewers need careful training. The selection should ideally be augmented by assessment centre exercises to add objectivity to the process.

## BEAUTY THAT IS MORE THAN SKIN-DEEP

Talented people will only be tempted if the offer is sufficiently attractive. Recruitment clearly depends upon an astute grasp of what motivates people. The organization should consider which of these motivators can realistically be delivered. As far as it can, it should change so that motivators can be provided. For example Holbeche (1998) reports that the term 'fast track' is appealing to many potential recruits. Providing a fast-track scheme is an example of how the organization can respond to attract the 'best' candidates in the job market.

Equally, however, the organization must acknowledge the limits to which it can satisfy people's needs. Not everyone can be on a fast track. It should use the recruitment process to instil realism and to be honest with people. This is not made any easier by graduates' unrealistic expectations.

Welch (1997) reports that the UK's Association of Graduate Recruiters carried out a survey that suggested that some 75 per cent of students expect to be treated as potential high-flyers. This seems patently unrealistic and organizations need to be quite clear at the outset what is on offer. Otherwise, they will end up being accused of having made false promises to people.

Buckley *et al.* (1998) describe the importance of making people's expectations more realistic. They see this as a means of reducing both the turnover and the lack of satisfaction and commitment caused by people's typical overestimates of what the organization might offer. They advocate giving people an honest preview of the career that is likely to be available to them. A case study of an organization being quite clear with people is provided by Arkin (1999) in her description of Tesco's approach. This supermarket chain has two recruitment streams for graduates. First, there is Excel, which is aimed at recruiting high-flyers into head office. Second, there is Select, which recruits people straight into stores. Those joining the second scheme are reported as knowing exactly what they are taking on and Arkin comments that 'such straight talking can only have a positive effect on retention' (p. 44).

It can be seen that organizations face the task of being attractive while also being honest. They must ensure that they are able to meet the needs of high-potential people. If necessary, the organization must change to be attractive. These people have to be offered promises and these promises have to be delivered. Otherwise, they will feel duped. Recruits of less potential also have needs to be met, but the organization must be honest and only make promises that are realistic.

The guiding principle for organizations should be that, in building a relationship that is based on trust, the starting point is to tell the truth from the outset. Unfortunately, the 'deal' in recruitment literature is often at odds with the picture that people perceive once they have joined. The contrast between the words at recruitment and the later 'truth' hardly gets the relationship off to a good start and might help account for high attrition rates among graduates. The organization needs to keep its promises to what it can deliver and then make sure it does deliver. If the organization has promised people challenge and responsibility they should be given challenge and responsibility.

In being honest, the problem that employers face is that this might lose good applicants to organizations making more grandiose promises. None the less, Holbeche (1998) describes the importance at the stage of recruitment of being honest about the speed of advancement. She says that while this might put off some highly ambitious people, it avoids the rapid loss of people who join only to find their progress is frustrated. Lawler (1994) goes further, saying 'the classic hierarchical striver whose idea of career success is upward mobility will not be attracted to a competency-based organization which stresses horizontal skill acquisition' (p. 12). However, it seems doubtful advice to put off all these people. If losing these strivers is not acceptable, the organization must change so that it can make promises of advancement that can be delivered. While it is vital to impart realism to most people, the organization will also want to recruit some highly talented people to become its future leadership. If ambition is part of the identity of such people, the organization will need to cater for it. That is, after all, the purpose of the restricted high-potential group.

Apart from being honest about the prospects, the organization needs to be honest about the nature of the work. Sims (1994) suggests the use of the *realistic job preview* (RJP) to inform people. Holton and Russell (1997) demonstrated that graduates who anticipated their job prior to employment were more committed than non-anticipators. Of course, the job that is previewed might be unattractive. If this is the case, the organization needs to change the work, not try to put the best gloss on it.

## CONVEYING COMMITMENT: WHEELING OUT THE BIG GUNS

Ghoshal and Bartlett (1998) draw attention to the importance of CEO involvement in the recruitment process. They describe how Bill Gates 'sees no activity as more important than meeting superior candidates to convince them that they should join Microsoft'. He invites summer interns in groups to his home. Ghoshal and Bartlett also quote the CEO of Enron, who asked 'how can we become a world-class company unless we have world-class people?', before throwing his weight behind the recruitment process.

Griffith (1998a) makes the same point using the case study of Apple. She describes how the CEO, Steve Jobs, says he spends a quarter of his time recruiting. Similarly, Al Zeien of Gillette is reported in the same article as saying that '40 per cent of his time is directed at finding the best people within and outside the company'. Griffiths reports that other companies who say their senior executives participate directly in recruitment include Citibank, and the food group General Mills.

This high-level involvement is clearly attractive to potential recruits. It reinforces the seriousness with which the organization takes building its talent and emphasizes that talent is a strategy for business success. CEO involvement also conveys the same message to those already in the organization. Conversely, a lack of CEO involvement conveys the message that implementing the HR strategy is not top priority. It can be left to the HR department.

## WAITING UNTIL YOU ARE SURE

A strategy of commitment and partnership implies that forming the relationship is done with the utmost care. Both sides need to maximize their information about each other. As Pfeffer (1994) observes, 'taking on people not readily eliminated exerts pressure to be careful and selective in hiring' (p. 32). He includes 'careful selection' among his 16 practices of good management.

Reichheld provides examples of the seriousness with which selection is taken from his case studies of what he sees as exemplary firms. One such firm is State Farms. It was reported by *Fortune* magazine as choosing its new insurance agents 'with the care one might give to choosing a spouse' (p. 112).

How should selection be carried out? In many circumstances, an assessment centre seems the best alternative. It gives maximum information on people (Ballantyne and Povah, 1995; Jansen and de Jongh, 1998; Woodruffe, 1993). The centre gets people to take part in exercises that simulate the demands that would be made of them if they were employed by the organization. For example, it might include writing a strategic review, a role play with a client and a group problem-solving meeting. Such centres are clearly applicable to graduate applicants and have the recruitment advantage of demonstrating to applicants the professionalism of the selection procedure. The organization is seen as both up to date and thorough. Candidates also feel they have been able to demonstrate their strengths, rather than being left with the feeling after an interview of having been able only to show a small part of themselves or the feeling after psychometric testing of mystification over what it was about.

The best exposure of all to someone is gained by their working within the organization for a while. The internships run by Proctor and Gamble (Donkin, 1998a) have already been described as a way of wooing people. They are also an extremely good way of gaining information about people. They last about 12 weeks during the summer between the second and third years of university. In a sense this is a marathon assessment centre in which the company and potential staff get to know each other very well indeed.

An assessment centre might not be applicable to all posts. For senior appointments, there might be the sense that it is inappropriate. In that case, the people making the appointment will need to gain maximum exposure to the candidate's track record. Certainly, it would be foolish to rely on an interview which tests behaviour in just one setting. At a senior level, exposure to the candidate is often vicarious and based on the person's reputation and track record.

The exposure to people needs to be relevant. It can be contrasted with the approach of simply 'getting close' to candidates by meeting them socially. As Donkin (1998c) amusingly observes of the executive who likes to get close to potential recruits by playing golf with them, this 'ensures that you get a golf-playing, male sycophant with a handicap one stroke away from your own'.

The objective should be to gain enough exposure so that each side is sure in their decision. The aim is to avoid the sense of having made a mistake that can come from either the employer or employee. Whitehead (1998) reports that the outplacement agency, Sanders & Sidney, found in a survey that one in 15 employees said they had been misplaced in the past year. Whitehead advises employees to be clear about what they want from a job and to find out about their prospective employer. It is in the organization's interest to help them do this and avoid a mistake. Mistakes cannot be afforded on the employer's side if a commitment has been made. If the employee feels they made a mistake and leaves, the cost is the loss of organizational investment and having to recruit the replacement. Whitehead (1998) reports that employers estimated that the average cost of failed appointments was £60 000 ($100 000).

This leads to clear advice on selection which is 'if in doubt do not appoint'. Whitehead's (1998) report of the Sanders & Sidney survey makes plain that employers should 'avoid expedient "best at the time" decisions'. In line with this advice, Prickett (1998d) reports that at least some employers would prefer not to fill all their graduate vacancies than to take on people lacking the necessary skills. This preference was reflected a year later in a report by Welch (1999) that described how employers in the UK's Association of Graduate Recruiters (AGR) had under-recruited by an average of 13 per cent 'instead of relaxing standards'.

The highly responsible behaviour of these organizations is thoroughly in accord with the principle of making sure that commitments are not made lightly. Organizations need to do all they can to avoid mistakes at selection. If a mistake has been made, it needs to be dealt with swiftly and decisively within the normal probation period.

## THE CHARISMATIC ORGANIZATION

The Enron case study as described by Ghoshal and Bartlett (1998) reveals an important aspect to recruitment, which is that success breeds success. Enron was transformed 'into one of the most exciting companies in the world' and now 'competes successfully for Harvard MBAs against McKinsey – the world's most attractive MBA employer'. But how do you turn the corner? The only obvious answers are to get organized, to be attractive by meeting people's needs, especially by showing commitment and to make wise and considered choices.

Above all, the organization needs to project a confidence to the world. While it is not possible to guarantee to people just where the organization will be going, it is surely important to convey that it will definitely be going somewhere. It is this confidence that conveys an idea of safety. In turn, this confidence might be the key to what makes the organization charismatic and able to attract people to an uncertain future.

Organizations would be well advised to check their image in the eyes of those they hope to recruit. They should then take the necessary remedial action. Highhouse *et al.* (1999) describe an approach to measuring 'company employment image'. It is based on identifying the dimensions that are salient to applicants, against which companies are subsequently measured.

## PEOPLE WHO CAN SHOW COMMITMENT

There is little point in recruiting people to the core who are unlikely to stay. This is an issue particularly in connection with retaining graduates, many of whom seem to view their first job as a way-station. It might be satisfactory to bring in such people as knowledge workers. However, they would not be the basis of a core for the future.

There are two ways forward if the organization wants to secure people in whom it can invest and whom it might hope to keep. One is to meet their needs, providing fast tracks and other motivators. However, to the extent that the culture of moving on is endemic in fresh graduates, one cannot help but sympathize with firms that feel they would be better off taking the second way. It is to let people get the need to move around out of their systems and recruit them at a slightly later stage. For example, Prickett (1998d) reports a survey showing that 40 per cent of those on the verge of graduating 'planned to spend less than two years with their first employer. Only 16 per cent expected to stay for at least five years.'

This is a very important decision. If it is true that changing jobs is a requirement for graduates to feel credible with their peers then organizations might be best advised to recruit their core after people have satisfied the need to make a move or two. However, it seems quite possible that the need for graduates to move around is brought about by the way in which they feel underutilized by their first employers, rather than being a matter of immutable fact. An organization might put itself at a great advantage if it recruits high-quality people and ensures that they stay by meeting their needs. This might include providing secondments to other organizations in a consortium to enable people to gain a varied experience.

## RECRUITING ON AN INTERNATIONAL SCALE

The international organization faces the question of whether high-potential people should be recruited globally or within the organization's 'home' country. The *IPD guide on international management development* (1997) makes clear that 'there is an increasing desire to develop local talent' (p. 31). Indeed, Shackleton and Newell (1997) see the recruitment of people on an international basis as a corollary of globalization. Pucik (1998) suggests that 'from a long-term perspective, a global organisation will have to be one in which it does not matter where people enter'. He cites Citicorp as a rare example of a global firm that has developed people from all continents and he adds this is only 'after several decades of effort'.

Organizations that follow this lead will have to undergo a transformation whereby posts that were traditionally expatriate are now filled by local high potentials. The *IPD guide* (1997) gives the example of Standard Chartered Bank. The bank is said to be aiming for a global network of locally hired high-potential people. This process is helped by the graduates being 'socialized' in a single global training centre for their first six months of employment.

As Shackleton and Newell point out, international recruitment means organizations being familiar with different recruitment customs. For example, the UK has the 'milkround system' under which employers visit universities to recruit graduates. On the other hand on the mainland of Europe the system of direct applications is encouraged. Without the campus visits, if an organization does not have a strong presence in one of these countries, it will be more difficult to attract direct applications from graduates.

To implement international recruitment, many organizations aim for an international cadre of talent. An issue they face is whether the mechanisms for choosing people externally and reviewing current employees' potential are decided and monitored centrally or locally. While it might theoretically be possible to thrive on anarchy, the risk is that a head office strategy is abandoned for local expediency. Apart from its other consequences this will mean there is no unifying competency standard that enables people to move between countries without question. An example of a company exerting central control is provided by the *IPD Guide on international management development* (1997). It describes how Unilever has a central 'high quality graduate' initiative which is controlled centrally. Each developed country in the Unilever Group 'is expected to contribute a particular percentage to the high quality graduate intake drawn from the top universities within those countries' (p. 27). The same guide also describes how Burmah Castrol aims to identify development potential throughout its units worldwide. The head office has the task of trying to avoid bureaucracy while limiting the subjectivity of a process of identifying potential that takes place through personal discussions and networking among managers.

Some sort of central control seems inevitable if the talent pool is to be seen as a group resource and a group strategy. Apart from any other consideration, a recruitment advantage of an international organization is the possibility of overseas experience. This will be facilitated by having a central input to ensure the strategy of gaining commitment by treating people as a resource is implemented internationally.

## FEEDBACK: RECRUITMENT INFLUENCING STRATEGY

Recruitment success or failure must feed back into the organization's strategy. In particular, the business strategy might have to be amended as a result of shortfalls in meeting recruitment targets. Williams and Dobson (1997) suggest that increasingly HRM will influence strategy through information on demographic changes and internal competencies.

A step on from this is for the organization to be opportunistic and amend business strategy around the people recruited rather than placing the emphasis the other way round. This might not suit every organization nor might it be suitable all the time. Nevertheless, for some, it might be appropriate to be continually looking out for talent, with a relatively open mind to people's precise specializations. Particular examples are provided by the City of London and Wall Street where the recruitment of 'stars' and teams of people could result in amendments to business strategy. Unfortunately, the corollary is that the loss of such people and teams might also mean amending strategy.

It is important to add that, if these opportunistic recruits are to be part of the core, they must possess the qualities that the organization needs for it to make a long-term commitment to them. Griffith (1998a) reports how Enron emphasizes finding 'talent' and then finding a position to suit the person, rather than finding people to suit positions. However, this talent will match the general requirements of Enron, and recruitment decisions will be guided by Enron's vision. Each organization needs to know the qualities that make up 'talent' for them, particularly the talent of the high-potential group. It is to these qualities that the next chapter turns.

# Selecting for the future: 11 making choices when you are not certain what you want

As the last chapter made clear, the strategy of commitment to people makes choosing them of paramount importance. They are joining for tomorrow as well as today and so the organization needs to satisfy itself that they match the requirements of the longer time frame as well as for the immediate future. When organizations want someone to join the talent pool, they need to find someone who will meet two targets. First, they will make an immediate contribution; second, they will have a continuing impact. If the organization wants the person to join the high potential group, a third target must be added. It is, arguably, the most important of all: that the person will become part of the future leadership.

In order to make judgements about people, the organization would like to know what is necessary for the future as well as the present. Immediately, it runs into the problem of the future being just a sketch.

## A SENSE OF UNCERTAINTY

The sketchiness of the future reflects the uncertainty with which it is viewed. By way of contrast, before giants had to try to learn to dance, specifying the qualities that made for future leadership appeared easy. Organizations were quite clear about what they wanted. 'Planning and organizing' was a ubiquitous competency, together with analytical skills and the ability to give direction. In short, competencies were about management and management was about command and control.

With hindsight, this certainty of what was required can be seen to have been an illusion based on an understandable failure to foresee changes in the environment. In particular, it neglected the increasing competitiveness of the market place and the related need to win customers' loyalty and then retain it. These changes have called for senior managers to behave towards staff in a way that will encourage and enable them to offer superior service to customers. This environment which led to delayering and teamwork has called for leaders with very different qualities – in particular the qualities of coach and enabler – in comparison to the command and control skills that dominated the past.

Of course, the wisdom of hindsight is marvellously easy and quite probably no one could have predicted the changes in the last quarter century. This is precisely the message that organizations have now taken on board: the only certainty is change and organizations have lost a feeling of knowing where they will be by the time they need the next generation of leaders.

The risk is that organizations will now overcompensate from their illusion of certainty in favour of a paralysis of uncertainty. They might be tempted to give up even having a strategy to grow their future leadership on the basis that they really do not know what sort of qualities will be needed. This would be an understandable but wrong reaction. Over-coming it requires organizations to think their way through what they hope to acquire in high-potential staff. However they approach the issue, one thing seems certain. People will need to be flexible and develop.

## AT LEAST YOU CAN BE SURE OF UNCERTAINTY

Hall and Mirvis (1995) place a great deal of emphasis on the need to be adaptable and to learn to learn. They see the crucial elements as being 'self-reflection or examining one's assumptions, testing out definitions of a situation, and being open to feedback' (p. 352). Hall and Fukami (1979) describe an effective person as possessing the 'longer-term functions of maintaining adaptability and a strong sense of identity' (p. 132). Hall and Mirvis (1995) define adaptability as 'learning how to be open to change' (p. 334) with identity being defined as 'gaining self-awareness and skills in self-management' (p. 334). Hall and Mirvis suggest it is people with the qualities of 'an appetite for continuous learning and the capacity to cope with the ambiguity and challenge of shifting job assignments' (p. 336) who should be hired as the 'few designated "high potential" employees' (p. 336).

To choose people who will be adaptable and learn to learn, organiza-tions need to know what behaviours to look for. Davis (1995) suggests that organizations will need people with a 'discipline of constant refinement' (p. 131) if they are to be the sort of people who will pursue learning and so enable their organizations to learn. He suggests that conscientiousness is particularly relevant. Jansen (1997) also believes attention needs to be directed at learning abilities. He specifies 'the ability (a) to construct models for seemingly fuzzy problems with many variables and (b) to put these hypotheses to an empirical test' (p. 139). Jansen notes how learning potential might be assessed by the increase in performance over two administrations of an assessment centre exercise, which seems a very practical idea.

One characteristic that seems clearly to be an asset to the adaptability of high potential staff is 'uncertainty orientation'. This is described by Sorrentino *et al.* (1995) as a motivation 'to learn from and incorporate new information in situations where there is uncertainty about the self and the environment' (p. 315).

McCall (1998) puts a great deal of emphasis on the qualities that enable a person to develop as the key to distinguishing 'high potentials from solid performers' (p. 126). He lists 11 qualities. These are reproduced in Table 11.1. McCall sees them as operating at different stages of a person learning from experience. One cluster (is committed to making a difference, is insightful, sees things from new angles and has the courage to take risks) is seen as giving the person the 'minimum criteria for being considered "high potential" and for having the opportunities to expand one's leadership repertoire' (p. 130). Another group (seeks opportunities to learn, adapts to cultural differences, seeks broad business knowledge and has the courage to take risks) provides a sense of adventure and gets the managers into developmental experiences. A third group (acts with integrity, brings out the best in people, seeks and uses feedback and is open to criticism) helps the person to create an effective context for learning. They 'create a setting in which other people are willing, perhaps eager to play a constructive role' (pp. 133–134) in the person's learning, and they cover the person being proactive in generating feedback on their impact and effectiveness. Finally, high potential people change as a result of experience and this relates to learning from mistakes and being open to criticism.

Choosing those who are flexible and able to develop implements the strategy by securing people who themselves are able to change rather than having to be changed as events unfold. It enables commitments to be made. It also means the organization is building and developing a resource of talented people.

## THE RIGHT TIME HORIZON

The ability to be flexible and to develop seems an unarguable quality for future high performers. Indeed Chapter 3 suggested a major aspect of talent is people's trainability and retrainability. However, quite obviously, there is more involved. In choosing people with talent and particularly with the potential to become future leaders, there are qualities over and

**Table 11.1**   Eleven Dimensions of early identification of global executives

1. **Seeks opportunities to learn.**
   Has demonstrated a pattern of learning over time. Seeks out experiences that may change perspective or provide an opportunity to learn new things. Takes advantage of opportunities to do new things when such opportunities come along. Has developed new skills and has changed over time.

2. **Acts with integrity.**
   Tells the truth and is described by others as honest. Is not self-promoting and consistently takes responsibility for his or her actions.

3. **Adapts to cultural differences.**
   Enjoys the challenge of working in and experiencing cultures different from his or her own. Is sensitive to cultural differences, works hard to understand them, and changes behaviour in response to them.

4. **Is committed to making a difference.**
   Demonstrates a strong commitment to the success of the organization and is willing to make personal sacrifices to contribute to that success. Seeks to have a positive impact on the business. Shows passion and commitment through a strong drive for results.

5. **Seeks broad business knowledge.**
   Has an understanding of the business that goes beyond his or her own limited area. Seeks to understand both the products or services and the financial aspects of the business. Seeks to understand how the various parts of the business fit together.

6. **Brings out the best in people.**
   Has a special talent with people that is evident in his or her ability to pull people together into highly effective teams. Is able to work with a wide variety of people, drawing the best out of them and achieving consensus in the face of disagreement.

7. **Is insightful: sees things from new angles.**
   Other people admire this person's intelligence, particularly his or her ability to ask insightful questions, identify the most important part of a problem or issue, and see things from a different perspective.

8. **Has the courage to take risks.**
   Will take a stand when others disagree, go against the status quo, persevere in the face of opposition. Has the courage to act when others hesitate and will take both personal and business risks.

9. **Seeks and uses feedback.**
   Pursues, responds to, and uses feedback. Actively asks for information on his or her impact and has changed as a result of such feedback.

10. **Learns from mistakes.**
    Is able to learn from mistakes. Changes direction when the current path is not working, responds to data without getting defensive, and starts again after setbacks.

11. **Is open to criticism.**
    Handles criticism effectively: does not act threatened or get overly defensive when others (especially superiors) are critical.

above flexibility. To decide what they are, a starting point is the current requirements for the role that the person is being selected to fill on entry. These can be specified in terms of the behaviours that are necessary for high performance in the role. For the high-potential group, the organization also needs the current specification of the leadership role to which they aspire.

The current requirements of the entry role and the leadership role must be oriented to the future, but it is the relatively immediate foreseeable future of the next three to five years and refers to what behaviours the organization needs from people for it to continue to be successful. The question is not 'what has made people successful in this role in the past?' It is 'what will make them successful in the future?' Here, Sparrow and Bognanno's (1993) distinction between competencies that are core, transitional, emerging and maturing is helpful. Core last throughout the period. Emerging become more important and maturing less important, while transitional help the organization make a change during the period. The organization needs people for the future with core and emerging competencies.

Many organizations stop there. The talent pool is chosen against the requirements for their entry role and the high-potential group is selected against the leadership profile. People match today's requirements and the future is safeguarded by ensuring that they are flexible and able to develop. Rather than over-engineering a process fraught with uncertainty, this might be seen as the best that can be achieved. On the other hand, there seems little to lose by trying to look beyond the current requirements of the current role and sketch in the requirements for the future role, particularly the next generation leadership role. This amended leadership role will then be the basis for bringing in high-potential staff. Again, they need to be flexible and able to develop if only because the vision of the future will be inaccurate and people need to align themselves with the future as it turns out rather than as it was forecast. The position is represented in Figure 11.1.

In choosing people to be the future leadership, the more that the organization can sketch in the requirements for that future role the better. As far as possible, the objective is to get away from bringing in people who will make an immediate contribution and assuming they will be appropriate for the future. Instead, the emphasis should be the opposite way round. Organizations need to bring in people for the future, if necessary making some sacrifice of the strongest possible immediate contribution.

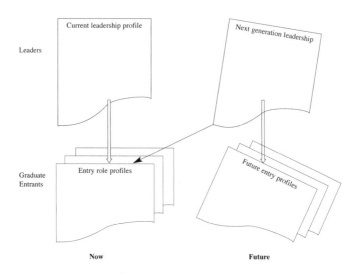

**Figure 11.1**    Current and future competency profiles

## A VISION OF THE FUTURE

To sketch in the requirements of future leaders, visioning is the critical starting point. This is true even if, as the cliché goes, the one thing that is certain is change itself. Under these circumstances, it is also certain that the vision far into the future will prove off-beam. Visions need updating and the further into the future, the hazier and more tentative the prediction will be. This should not lead organizations to drop out of the visioning business. Without a vision, you are bound to be wrong. A vision that is constantly updated at least stands a chance of coming in correct at the end.

In moving from the vision to the qualities that are required in future leaders, the 'classic' approach is to proceed via the business strategy and finish with the people. The links between the vision, the business strategy and the HR strategy are conceptualized as a linear progression. For example, Brake (1997) describes the process as starting with 'a compelling vision of the future' (p. 31). Only then, can the organization go on to answer 'what type of men and women do we need to fulfill our global vision and implement our global strategies?' (p. 31).

The business strategy might be conceived in terms of organizational competencies. Hamel and Prahalad (1994) describe the process of having industry foresight to determine the new types of customer benefit the organization should seek to provide in 5, 10 or 15 years. The subsequent question is what organizational competencies will be needed to offer those benefits. The process of working from the organizational competencies to the people has been labelled 'skill-based planning' by Hirsh and Reilly, (1998). They describe this as starting with an identification of 'what the business needs to be good at – its organisational capabilities' (p. 38). This is then linked to what will be required of people. These people requirements are much more than technical and professional skills. They are the skills required to exploit the technical and professional competencies.

At first sight, the process seems quite simple. Vision the future, set the business strategy and then set about recruiting the type of staff to implement that strategy. However, this linear model might not be entirely accurate. First, the vision of the future which sets the business strategy will have obvious direct implications for the required leadership qualities. For example, the retailer's vision might be a future in which customers do not visit stores physically but via the Internet. The resulting virtual retailers will be very different organizations from the chain of stores of today, and certainly they will require fewer people who are gifted at being leaders of store staff. Their leaders might, instead, need to be exceptionally good at analysing sales and pricing data. Both the business strategy and the leadership flow from the same vision coincidentally rather than sequentially. Second, the leadership might well be the business strategy. The business strategy is to beat the competition by attracting and then developing and retaining the best people as staff and leaders.

In short, the linear model alone – vision, then strategy, then leadership – might be rather simplistic. Business strategy and leadership are inseparable. Both are strongly and jointly influenced by the organization's vision of the environment within which it will be operating and how it will be succeeding in that environment.

## FROM VISION TO POTENTIAL

The longer-term vision might point up qualities that future leaders are expected to require that are different from those needed by current leaders because of envisaged changes in the environment and the way work is organized. However, it must be stressed that forecasting competencies far into the future is bound to be attended by uncertainty. Rather than attempting to specify them in detail, the more practical way forward that is advocated here is to specify the current competencies and then examine them against the distant vision and make amendments.

One way of presenting competencies is to show the behaviours needed for each of several levels of each competency. An example of an extract from such a competency framework is contained in Table 11.2. For each role, the competencies and levels are then specified to form a profile for the role. Comparing profiles shows the 'gap' between roles.

The competency approach has wide currency as a way of specifying the behaviours that an organization needs its people to possess. Competencies are the behaviours that people need to be able to demonstrate in the various situations they are confronted with at work. The fact that competencies should and can be oriented into the future seems lost on some of their critics. For example, McCall (1998) describes how either a competency or a trait approach results in 'a list (of attributes or behaviors) based on the past or current state of affairs (either job demands or successful people)' (p. 120). Likewise Antonacopoulou and FitzGerald (1996) declare that 'instead of growing dynamic, flexible and adaptable managers, capable of facing the challenges of tomorrow, the risk seems to be that the competency framework is, in an evolving society, cultivating dinosaurs struggling to develop the skills of the past' (p. 34). In fact, there is nothing intrinsic in the approach that roots it in the past or present. Indeed, there is every reason to ensure that the current specification of competencies is oriented to the immediate future. It will then serve as a basis for selecting and developing people who will enable the organization to implement its business strategy successfully.

The future is taken into account even more obviously when the more distant vision is used to amend the current specification of the leadership role and write the next generation leadership role. With a next generation orientation, the competencies attempt to specify the behaviours that will eventually be needed by the future leadership of the organization. In specifying behaviours required in the future, McCall is quite right in saying that competencies specify the end-state. However, this is not a penetrating criticism of competencies. Once specified, the end-state competencies need to be examined and judgements made on which behaviours will be developed in the person's career and which are needed at the outset, at least in embryonic form. For example, the behaviour 'adopts a corporate perspective' can be developed. On the other hand, 'produces creative/innovative solutions' appears a quality the person will need to start out with. Finally, some specific behaviours eventually needed in the organization will need to be backtracked to a more general form. An example of this process is provided by Church and Waclawski (1998). They found that people who show the behaviours of transformational leadership are more innovative and intuitive. If transformational leadership is the end-state, people need to start out with the behaviours of innovation and intuition. The difference is clear. If you are looking to bring in a new general manager to start work next week, it is the current

**Table 11.2** Example section of a competency framework

| Example competencies | Example behaviours | | |
| --- | --- | --- | --- |
| | Level 1 | Level 2 | Level 3 |
| Flexibility | Accepts and follows revised instructions Is willing to adapt to changing circumstances | Is willing to take on new responsibilities Handles ambiguity of practices and processes Effectively implements changes within own team | Actively promotes change Uses innovation and creativity to develop strategy |
| Communication | Listens and pays attention to others Communicates clearly orally and in writing | Tailors oral and written communication to audience Recognizes sensitivity of communicating information | Presents arguments based on sound reasoning Facilitates agreements through an awareness of others' needs |
| Achieves results | Organizes own work in an efficient way Ensures own tasks are completed as requested | Sets objectives, targets and deadlines Plans allocation of work Monitors and reviews activities | Develops long-term strategic plans Reviews effectiveness of strategies |
| Breadth of perspective | Has an interest in issues facing own department Is aware of the organization's aims Recognizes the effect of own input into the department | Seeks to understand other departments' aims and objectives Considers the demands of a competitive environment Recognizes the impact team performance has on profits | Shows awareness of corporate impact of outside events Considers wide variety of factors e.g. political, economic |

leadership competencies of today that matter. If you are bringing in a graduate to evolve into a general manager it is potential to acquire the next generation leadership competencies that is required.

We end up then with a competency framework for current roles, together with the amendments necessary for next generation leadership potential. The competency framework can be used to integrate the HR process. The competencies are used to select people for today's roles and to manage people in the present. For example, the competencies of today are used to decide if someone is ready to occupy today's leadership role and to give people 360° feedback in terms of today's behaviours. The next generation leader's competencies set a development agenda for people in the high-potential group. They are also the competencies that are needed for entry to the high-potential group. The integrative function of competencies is illustrated in Figure 11.2 which shows the uses to which a framework can be put.

## GENERIC OR TAILORED

In defining long-term potential, we are likely to arrive at a position whereby there will be considerable overlap in the leadership qualities required by different organizations. However, it is a major step simply to use a generic list of competencies as the basis for specifying potential. First, variations in the qualities required will occur between organizations in different sectors. As an example, professionals and professional firms are likely to require a 'light touch' type of leadership. Indeed, Jain and Triandis (1997) subtitle their book on management in research and development organizations 'managing the unmanageable'. On the other hand, a more

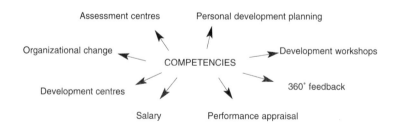

**Figure 11.2**   Competencies integrate HR

visible and involved style might be appropriate for less individualistic groups of staff. Schneider (1987) points out that research on leadership effectiveness bears out his prediction 'that different kinds of people are likely to be effective leaders in different kinds of organizations' (p. 449).

Second, even within a sector, a specific list can incorporate the values and culture of the specific organization. It achieves a much greater sense of ownership. Anyone who has derived a tailor-made list for an organization will know how organizations have their own language which subtly conveys their priorities in their own code. All this would be lost with a generic list.

Third, if the competencies are to help the organization achieve its tailor-made strategy, they too should be tailor-made. Indeed the use of a generic list goes against the whole notion described, for example, by Lado and Wilson (1994), of gaining competitive advantage by building a set of unique competencies which mark the organization out as different. As these writers say, the goal is to achieve a match between the characteristics of managers and the requirements of organizational strategy.

Fourth, even if the strategy was very similar, an organization will not set itself apart by having the same competencies as its competitors. It needs the specific list to enable it to try to set itself apart in terms of its leadership and management rather than being just like its competitors.

Fifth, there is a problem of knowing which of the legion of lists to choose and the paradox is that one will only know if a borrowed list is reasonably accurate by deriving a tailored list to check it against.

## Selecting for organizational membership

While these are all good reasons for a tailored list of requirements, perhaps the strongest reason is that people are being selected for a long-term membership of a particular organization. Some writers (e.g. Seegers, 1997) nowadays make this the pre-eminent point and suggest that selection should focus on finding people for organizational membership. In selecting for the organization, Lawler (1994) says one is particularly looking for 'individuals who fit the learning environment that is provided by the organization. ... The selection process needs to focus on identifying people who can learn and follow the various career tracks that are available in the organization' (p. 9). The approach is also advocated by De Geus (1997). He says that, in companies which have a long-term future, 'recruits are judged as much on the basis of their fit with the company's values and principles as they are on their ability to fulfill the technical requirements of the job' (p. 59). Given the uncertainties of the future, if organizations are recruiting for the longer term, they are, almost by definition, recruiting people to be organizational members rather than for some particular jobs.

Pfeffer (1998) also suggests that selection procedures should be used primarily to discover a person's fit with the organization. He points out that this is a better use of time than asking a series of questions to test the brainpower of MBA students from major business schools, when these people are 'obviously talented, motivated and very intelligent' (p. 72).

The organization, then is aiming to select members who are similar in terms of the values they share. These values need to be reflected in the competencies. For example, if the value is to be open and honest, this needs to be within the competency framework. Aside from those competency behaviours that directly reflect the values, organization members also need to be similar in terms of the other competencies. The members will all have talent. This does, however, carry an obvious risk. It is that the organization becomes stereotyped and vulnerable to changes in the environment. It is vitally important to select people who form a range on everything other than the agreed values and competencies. This range is needed to cover possible futures and to allow for the innovation that comes from different approaches to an issue.

Obviously, having competencies and values in common places a restriction on diversity, but it is a restriction that seems common sense. It seems natural that one will not be aiming for diversity on qualities that have been specifically agreed as necessary for success. For example, it would be bizarre to have diversity on problem-solving ability or self-responsibility. However, aside from the competencies and values, the organization should aim for diversity.

## WHAT DO OTHERS THINK?

Although organizations should derive their own lists of competencies, it is helpful to check these against the 'conventional wisdom' of what will be required for the future. They can then make a conscious decision to incorporate other people's ideas of which attributes are seen as being important for the future. These ideas should be used to prime an organization's thinking about its own requirements and should not be used as a definitive list. They are considered under the two main headings of cognitive and interpersonal skills.

## COGNITIVE SKILLS

Cognitive skills that are likely to be important for most organizations cover reasoning ability and innovation. Pickard (1997c) reports that Warren Bennis offered her the opinion in an interview that 'in a knowledge workers' society, we will need leaders at every level who are extraordinarily brainy'. Jansen (1997) agrees, and argues that the general effect of new technologies is likely to be upgrading, not deskilling, because people will have to interact with the technologies. He identifies being intelligent among the general characteristics that will be required in the future and likens this to the 'supra competency' which Dulewicz (1989) labelled as being 'intellectual'.

Conger (1998) speculates that people will need 'marketplace capabilities'. These feature the ability to handle change outside the organization. They will demand long-range thinking. He suggests managers 'will be under far greater pressure to look long-range, to envisage alternative scenarios in an uncertain world'. Visioning and strategic thinking are among the top five qualities Rajan and van Eupen (1997) report from interviews with 49 top business leaders from the UK's service sector.

Aside from being able to think an issue through, people are also likely to need the cognitive skill of creativity. Innovation, or the ability to generate novel ideas is included in the *IPD guide on international management development* list of global core competencies. O'Neill (1997) says, if the organization is undergoing radical change and transformation it will need people who 'think the unthinkable'. He links this to being innovators in terms of the distinction of adaptors versus innovators (Kirton, 1976, 1994).

## INTERPERSONAL SKILLS

### Emotional maturity and self-confidence

Yukl and van Fleet (1992) cite as key requirements emotional maturity and self-confidence. They are related to the emotional intelligence traits popularized by Goleman (1998). He describes this type of intelligence in terms of a person's ability to restrain negative feelings like self-doubt and anger and instead to concentrate on the more positive characteristics of being affable, resilient and optimistic. Davies *et al.* (1998) say that much of what is meant by emotional intelligence is covered by 'well-known personality factors' (p. 1012). What might be new is the factor of 'emotion perception'. In general, then, emotional intelligence is better seen as a label than a discovery. Nevertheless, it is clear that Davies *et al.* and Goleman agree that the empathy covered by emotional intelligence will provide people with the ability to understand people's needs and provide constructive feedback.

## Transformational leadership

As well as the market-place capabilities discussed earlier, Conger (1998) describes the need for 'organizational capabilities'. These cover the leader's task to 'motivate and inspire employees who view themselves as less dependent on their organisations'. This task is likely to be met by being transformational. These transformational skills have been described by Bass and Avolio (1990) and include giving individualized concern, giving frequent reward and providing intellectual stimulation.

## Integrity

The ability to inspire trust and motivation was the top priority of 49 business leaders from the UK's service sector interviewed by Rajan and van Eupen (1997). McGuire (1998) describes the need for sensitivity to win people's loyalty and authenticity for long-term respect. Integrity is also mentioned by Yukl and van Fleet (1992) in their list of requirements.

## Collaborative skills

Miles and Snow (1996) argue that in third-wave, networked, organizations a new set of competencies is needed to replace the general manager competencies of the divisionalized firm. Third-wave competencies are concerned with collaborative knowledge and skills. Hamel and Prahalad (1994) also discuss how the ability to work in coalitions will be part of the competency set of tomorrow. It 'entails a careful balancing of competitive and cooperative agendas over time' (p. 211). They see these skills as necessary because organizations will need to maximize their share of influence over industry development and this means forming coalitions.

## Influencing skills

Jansen (1997) singles out people's capacity to negotiate as of critical importance in the future. This is because organizations will be increasingly flexible and dynamic. In these conditions 'employees have to manage a complex set of interfaces with different environments – with their "subordinates", with external or internal customers, with financial stakeholders, with suppliers, with political institutions and so on' (p. 131). Davis (1995) also suggests that leadership will need to be exercised through persuasion and example and interpersonal relationships will be of increasing importance.

## Cultural Sensitivity

Cultural empathy is also among the 'selection considerations' listed by the *IPD guide on international management development* (1997). Donkin (1998e) reports that sensitivity in different cultures was one of the qualities revealed in a survey of the qualities most seen by chief executives as needed in successors. The survey was by the London Business School and the Association of Executive Search Consultants.

## Conclusion

These ideas of others are food for thought. They are not a substitute for deriving a tailor-made list of competencies. They might, however, contribute to it.

## CONFLICT BETWEEN THE REQUIREMENTS OF IMMEDIATE AND FUTURE ROLES

There might be a conflict between the competencies people need on entry and later in their careers. For example, later on the person might need to take an overview, but early in their careers working with detail might be important. Likewise, later on a questioning attitude might be needed in contrast to a more compliant initial response.

These conflicts need to be acknowledged. Otherwise, the person brought in with the qualities for the future will become either frustrated or rejected early in their career. Acknowledgement of the conflict can take two forms. The first is to change the nature of the person's initial work so it is more congruent with the qualities they will need in the future. The second is to make the person aware that there is indeed a conflict and for both sides to make allowances during the period it exists.

The scale of the conflict between present and future requirements is unlikely to be large. Much of what organizations need from high potential people in the future should also enable them to make an immediate contribution. For example, the future strategic thinker will be today's analytic problem solver.

## FEEDBACK INTO STRATEGY

The relationship between specifying a strategy and developing the competencies to implement it is not one-way. As Seegers (1997) points out, the strategy will need to be adapted if there is little prospect of developing the required competencies in time. Likewise, Lawler (1994) observes that 'it does not make sense for an organization to launch a particular business strategy if it is unlikely to be able to develop the competencies to implement it and bring it to fruition' (p. 12).

The more radical possibility is to go further and base the strategy around the competencies rather than simply taking the competencies into account. Advancing this model, Snow and Snell (1993) comment that in future it may be 'more prudent to assume that the workforce is essentially fixed and that competitive strategy is a more adjustable element of the company' (p. 460). The foundation of the strategy is the quality of human capital and rather than a single set of core competencies, the objective is to develop 'a broad skill base for value creation' (p. 462). The choice of basing the business strategy around the people rather than the people around the strategy builds in a strong commitment to members of the organization. In order for it to work, people have to develop so that they are capable of delivering a business strategy that will be successful.

# Development: making the most of people     12

---

Some executives in organizations behave as if development should not be needed. Their attitude is that you hire people up and running rather than developing them. It is up to the people themselves to keep up to date. If they become obsolete someone new is found to replace them. Such an approach is clearly the opposite of a strategy of partnership and commitment. It is a naked form of the contingent and disposable attitude to staff. It only bears close scrutiny in the case of hiring people with a track record for the short term.

If a longer-term relationship is wanted, it is bound to involve a commitment by the organization to people's development. Failing to invest in people's ongoing development almost inevitably means that gradually their value will diminish and so they will offer the organization less. For people without experience, the arguments are all the more obvious. If high-potential staff are seen as a strategic response to the future, it is axiomatic that one nurtures them to increase their value and preparation.

The act of development is a key part of implementing the strategy of partnership and commitment to people. A partnership approach to development is well summed up by Ciba, whose management development mission is the 'identification, development and deployment of management potential in line with business objectives and employee aspirations' (Currie, 1998). De Geus (1997) describes how in companies bound by mutual trust, 'individuals understand that in exchange for their effort and commitment, the company will help them develop their potential' (p. 58). He says that 'managers who want to build an organization that can survive many generations pay attention to the development of employees above all other considerations' (p. 57). The objective is to help people develop to ensure their employability within the organization, not outside it. The internal focus of employability seems to be that adopted by Rank Xerox, whose 3D programme – define, decide, develop – is described by Wills (1997). In this programme, staff can obtain the competency list for the job to which they aspire and tailor their development accordingly.

Development not only helps to build and maintain a resource for the future. It is essential to retain people in the present. It is most unlikely that good people will simply wait until they become outdated through lack of development. They will leave well before that happens. Nowadays development is high on people's agenda and if they feel neglected they will move elsewhere. Prickett (1998b) reports that London University's survey of graduates found that over 90 per cent 'expect their employer to help their development'. Holbeche (1998) found that a third of her sample of high-flyers would leave if they could not broaden their skills. An illustrative cautionary tale is provided by McCall (1998). He reports, 'one individual found himself trapped by his own accomplishments in a sequence of jobs within the same technical speciality. ... Eventually, he resigned and went to work somewhere else where he could broaden his experience' (p. 156). There are three key questions to answer in looking at the development of high-potential staff. They are:

- What are you trying to develop?
- How does the development take place?
- Who is responsible for it?

## WHAT ARE YOU TRYING TO DEVELOP?

The straightforward answer is that development should be focusing on the competencies that will be required for the future. The idea of development is to convert people's potential into an actual capability to behave in line with the competencies. The person with critical reasoning develops into a strategic thinker. The interpersonally skilled person develops into a transformational leader. An approach that is an alternative to focusing on competencies is to think about the situations that the person will need to be able to deal with successfully. This is the approach favoured by McCall. He says that the executive development programme must be derived directly from business strategy and prepare executives to deal with the challenges they will face under the strategy. Uncertainty is just another challenge. Thus, he says, 'even if the business environment is largely unpredictable, making specific strategies impossible to determine, there must at least be a strategy for dealing with the uncertainty' (p. 97).

McCall's approach lends a helpful focus to development. It can be seen as complementary to competencies. The competencies should be the behaviours that will enable the person to meet the future challenges. However, the advantage of the competency approach is that competencies have a broader application than a set of challenges that may never come about. The person will have developed competencies that might well be useful even if the challenges turn out to be different from those expected. Preparing for future challenges might be a more accessible way of viewing development, but competencies offer a more robust currency than only focusing on specific future challenges.

## HOW DOES THE DEVELOPMENT TAKE PLACE?

### Stage one: awareness and planning

The 'how' of development must start with how the person becomes aware that there is something he or she needs to develop. Although, conceivably, development might happen without awareness, just from being in situations, it seems far more likely to occur if the person goes into situations with a view to gaining development and comes out of them reflecting on what has been achieved developmentally.

The classic time to review what needs to be developed is, of course, at appraisal. However, equally clearly development is not, or should not be, a once-a-year issue. Seegers (1997) describes how management development should nowadays be seen as a continuous process. It involves assessing the organization's future requirements and its employees' capability of meeting them, coupled with the necessary development to make up any shortfall. Furthermore, developmental discussions are probably not best carried out at the same time as an appraisal that might influence salary. Most people are bound to be defensive if they feel that acknowledging or even revealing a development need might affect their pay.

The appraisal should culminate in a development plan. Seeing that it is the plan rather than the appraisal that really is crucial, organizations have looked for other and perhaps better ways of arriving at a plan. One possibility is 360° feedback. Another is to use a development centre (Woodruffe, 1993) where people get feedback on their display of the competencies.

It is important that the development plan is a collaboration between the person and the organization. It needs to be based around the requirements of the present role or a future role (the 'what' of development). Furthermore, the plan itself (the 'how') will need the involvement of line management who, after all, has to 'pay' for it in terms of either a budget or time. It might also benefit from the expertise of an HR professional who can see, creatively, how development needs might be addressed.

Each person's development plan should be based around their own particular needs. Seegers (1997) contrasts this with a systems approach, which he sees as outmoded by its very methodical nature. For example, there is what he calls the 'formalistic management development system' which 'amounts to a cram course for a line or staff career' (p. 584). It lets graduates know what to expect in terms of jobs and training in their first six years. Alternatively, there is the, again outmoded, 'breeding ground model'. Under this approach graduates are 'hired as "supernumeraries"' (p. 586). Seegers describes the problem with these models as being that they are not based 'on the individual's pattern of growth and needs' (p. 586). He comments that it is questionable 'whether people with *real* talent will have the patience to wait six to eight years before being allowed to show what they can do' (p. 586).

## Stage two: implementation

### Experiences at work

There is a fundamental split between on-the-job experience and other experiences as the means to bring about development. McCall puts all his emphasis on the former. He says that 'most of the development described by successful executives occurred through on-the-job experiences' (p. 62). Mirvis and Hall (1996b) also declare that 'the best development occurs on the job' (p. 83). Having specified the future challenges, McCall believes the task of the organization is to find the experiences to help people prepare to meet the challenges. As an example he cites the corporation with the strategy of sustained growth. This gives rise to such challenges as being able to 'deal effectively with increased complexity resulting from growth' (p. 102). Experiences that might help develop the ability to meet the challenge include adapting a business to a new country and leading a turnaround that requires changing the direction of an operation. Those who prefer to think in terms of competencies can use the same analysis, with the purpose of development being to acquire the competencies by exposure to the necessary experiences.

McCall groups developmental experiences under the headings of:

- **Assignments**   An example is fixing/stabilizing a failing situation
- **Hardships**   An example is having a deal that fell part. As McCall points out, such experiences 'are not amenable, physically or morally, to organizational manipulation for developmental purposes' (p. 74)
- **Other people**   Examples are superiors with exceptional (good or bad) qualities

In addition to these experiences, Holbeche (1998) singles out the experience of dealing with organizational politics as being of particular value.

## You cannot beat a challenge

There is a good deal of agreement that people find most impact in experiences that involve a high level of coping with adversity. The point is made by McCall (1998) and Holbeche (1998) found in her survey of high-flyers that 'being thrown in at the deep end' (p. 38) was the most cited 'greatest learning experience'. The general point is also made by Rajan and van Eupen's (1997) survey of UK business leaders, many of whom had memorable experiences in their formative years. These included personal crises, such as the death of a parent. Again, Donkin (1998b) reports that David Norburn, director of Imperial College Management School in London, carried out a detailed survey of directors of large companies in the UK and USA. He found that the more successful directors were distinguished from the less successful by their experiences between ages 25 and 35. Holbeche concludes that it is not so much the particular experience or other opportunity that enables development but the sense of achievement that those experiences give.

Storey, *et al.* (1997) also acknowledge the power of 'challenging assignments' in their comparison of management development in Japan and the UK. The difference between the nations was that the Japanese had a more systematic approach to development compared to the British reliance on luck. One way of being more systematic is to follow McCall's recommendation and carry out an audit of the skills that are likely to be developed by working in different parts of the organization. For example, working in the finance function might develop analysis and strategic thinking whereas a growth-oriented division might teach getting results and flexibility. This audit or profiling process will reveal which skills are hard to develop anywhere in the organization, in which case McCall suggests creating the required 'school' rather than relying forever on bringing in from outside people with the skill.

In providing people with these developmental experiences, organizations can benefit from McCall's advice on helping people get the most developmental impact from them. People need high quality feedback to identify what they need to develop. They then need resources and support to help them change. The focus is on enabling people to learn and develop and so the organization needs to be tolerant of the errors involved during the time that the person is learning by trial and error. The idea is not to punish people for mistakes or engage in some form of 'destruction testing'.

## The challenge of a transfer

Rajan and van Eupen include frequent job transfers in their suggestions for experiences that will expand the horizons of potential leaders. The transfers will probably be within the person's own organization, but Holbeche (1998) describes how some organizations cooperate in a network. People from any one organization are seconded to others in the network to broaden their experience.

## Going abroad

A particular form of transfer that is mentioned by many writers is the international assignment. For example, Professor Norburn was reported by Donkin (1998b) as contending that international exposure was the second factor alongside experiences between ages 25 and 35 that distinguished successful directors of UK and US large companies.

Pucik (1998) observes that for global organizations, a major element of development is creating a global mindset. He advocates 'cross-border job swaps or assignments to multicultural task forces and project teams'. He stresses how important developing networks is to future leaders. Gillette appears to be an example of a company following this approach. The CEO, Al Zeien, is reported by Griffith (1998b) to move people between countries and divisions to make sure managers worldwide are on the same wavelength. Mr Zeien sees this movement as placing people in the role of 'idea ambassadors' who can transfer concepts.

Gillette's use of the expatriate as an ambassador is one of two models of the expatriate assignment discussed by Pucik. He contrasts this model of the headquarter's teacher going out to the empire with the model of the expatriate going out as a student. An organization that seems to use the student model is Cable and Wireless. Maitland, (1998c) describes their programme called Leaders of Tomorrow. It identifies and tracks people a 'few steps from the top' and sends them on international assignments to gain experience. SmithKline Beecham is another company reported by Maitland (1998c) using the student model. It requires potential general managers to have experience of two countries, two functions and two sectors. A final example is Ciba. Currie (1998) describes how they see the need for people to develop personal international management expertise through international assignments.

The two models of being a student and teacher can be seen as applying to the two important target groups for expatriation that are discussed by the UK's IPD in a *Guide on international management development* (1997). The groups are:

- **Young managers**   For this group the guide says, 'when posting a high potential the company often tends to be rather less interested in the improved performance of its foreign operating unit … but regards the posting as a long-term investment in an individual' (p. 25). The guide gives the example of British Airways, for whom 'international assignments are now part of the graduate training programme, giving a clear message that foreign experience is essential for career development' (p. 29).

- **Senior executives**   For these people the assignment 'serves as a final preparation for an important corporate position and/or to coach foreign managers and develop local expertise' (p. 25).

Despite the value of the experience, there are caveats to being an overseas executive, as the article by Maitland (1998c) makes clear. First, people overseas can miss out on having a view on the strategic direction of the business and on the threats and opportunities it faces from technology and market changes. This lack of view will preclude them getting top jobs. Second, they can suffer from a 'behavioural detachment' after working in a local culture that is inappropriate for or misunderstood by headquarters. It is clearly important that the organization actively combats these two issues. Failing to do so might prompt the person to move on. Indeed, Maitland reports a US study that found that over a quarter of managers were actively looking to change companies on their return from overseas.

An additional source of caution is the possibility of the failed assignment. The cost of this is enormous. Shaffer and Harrison (1998) quote estimates that range from direct costs of each failure being between $55 000 and $250 000, with a top estimate of $1 million as the cost of early termination.

In the light of the statistics and problems, it is clear the process of international assignment needs to be managed carefully. Maitland (1998c) reports how SmithKline Beecham 'handles the issue by rigorously planning international careers'. The head of HR describes losing high potential people as a very rare occurrence.

An aspect to this management is the family and spouse's adjustment to the assignment. Shaffer and Harrison found that such non-work factors were more important than work factors for managers with greater family responsibilities. They recommend providing families with realistic previews as well as language training and the means to keep in touch with people back home, via, for example, e-mail and video conferencing facilities.

Pucik (1998) notes how sociocultural trends, such as dual career families, are creating additional, difficulties for international assignments and argues that people will need to undertake them relatively early in their careers before they have these constraints. However, some organizations are seemingly more ready to be responsive than others. In an interview with Al Zeien, CEO at Gillette, Griffith (1998b) reports that managers with that company should expect to be relocated three or four times in their first dozen years. The CEO is reported as saying that people in dual career marriages probably should not work for Gillette.

## Off-the-job experiences

It can be concluded that there is a raft of experiences at work that can bring about development. Aside from these possibilities, development might also be encouraged by formal courses, which complement or supplement on-the-job experiences. In addition, experiences outside work, such as voluntary activities, might also be developmental. McCall sees the role of formal courses and non-work experiences as being to make up for experiences that cannot be gained as part of the job. He says that 'training can be used as a substitute for experiences that are not widely available or are too risky for "rookies"' (p. 79).

There is much to be said for this tilting the balance in favour of work experience. In particular, it has the advantage that line management can see that development on the job is also getting the job done and is therefore relevant to the business. On the other hand, developmental options that are not wholly on the job might deserve slightly greater consideration than given by McCall. There are nowadays quite imaginative solutions to the vexed issue of ensuring business relevance. For example, a development centre can simulate difficult situations that are encountered in the work role and give the participant a chance to practise and get feedback. One example is provided by Woodruffe and Wylie (1994) in their description of development centres at NatWest Group. Another is given by Refaussé (1996) who describes a development centre at Allied Domecq. As both articles suggest, development centres typically include sessions which enable people to gain insights on their career priorities as well as considering feedback on where their strengths lie. Relevance can also be built into workshops that are designed to focus on particular competencies and help the person learn the behaviours needed for high performance in terms of the competency.

Assignment and project work can also be made to address real business problems. They are then far more likely to be taken seriously by, and meet with the encouragement of, senior management than if they seem irrelevant to the business. An interesting case study of the use of project work is provided by the *IPD guide on international management development* (1997).

It describes Deutsche Bank's Pan-European project groups. The initiative targets high potentials in the age range 30–40. They work on projects with a European dimension over six months, having been presented with the projects by senior managers at a seminar. One topic, for example, was 'Pan-European Cash Management'. This type of project addresses business needs and helps the person develop at the same time. The meeting of business needs while achieving personal development is also discussed by Mirvis and Hall (1996b). They describe the inclusion in action learning programmes of projects that emphasize adaptive skills. They cite 3M, Motorola and GE as companies that have incorporated personal development into work projects. They also describe how 'Eli Lilly has for years utilized real-work projects, often related to a total quality or continuous improvement process' (p. 83).

Apart from becoming more relevant, off-the-job development activities have also been made briefer. Authers (1998) describes how the Advanced Management Programmes (AMPs) used to be 'finishing schools for high-flying executives just before they graduate to the board' and perhaps lasting three months. Nowadays, such programmes tend to be shorter and more flexible, with a major benefit being the other people whom participants meet.

Bradshaw (1998a) reports the growing number of briefer management courses in the USA and Europe 'aimed specifically at high potential young managers'. They are designed for people who do not want to engage in a long formal course. They build upon the experiences that the person gains at work. Pitfield (1998) reports that business schools are offering programmes to slot in before an MBA and which will provide a '"stepladder" of qualifications'. He cites the example of Darden, a US business school 'that has designed a special programme for young, high potential managers with between five and 10 years' work experience'.

Then there is the MBA itself. Quite apart from being a means of development, MBAs might be expected by high potential staff and therefore act as a prerequisite for retaining them. The popularity of doing an MBA is attested to by Holbeche's (1998) survey. She found that half the people surveyed had updated their qualifications since joining their present employer and that the majority of the people who have updated have done so by gaining an MBA. However, she cautions that 'one of the commonest complaints made by high flyers who had taken their MBA is that their organisation did not specifically use the enhanced skills and knowledge arising from the studies' (pp. 41–42). Clearly, organizations cannot retain people simply by writing the cheque for the MBA. They must value the input that the person brings back from the business school.

As regards the relevance of an MBA, Professor Norburn of Imperial

College is reported by Donkin (1998b) as believing in more emphasis being put on simulations and projects which will stretch people. These projects could be carried out within the organization. Indeed, the entire MBA can be either in-house or tailored for a particular company. Bradshaw (1998c) describes an advantage of these over the public version as being that companies 'can reward their high-flying staff, and so prevent defections to rival companies, while controlling the timing of the programme'. She says the phenomenon is largely European and that 'US business schools have found the concept hard to swallow'. Examples of companies in Europe with company-sponsored MBAs include Arthur Andersen, the BBC, British Airways and Cable and Wireless. On the other hand, the USA is reported by Pitfield (1998) to have pioneered the concept of a corporate university. This will also achieve the objective of relevance to the business and it is an approach that has taken off in the USA and has now crossed to the UK.

The problem with in-house MBAs is their perceived lack of portability, which can make them of less interest to people. Paradoxically, to retain people, they need to be offered development that will enable them to leave. The currency of development offered by an employer has to be acceptable elsewhere. In order to achieve this organizations might 'benchmark' their in-house courses and workshops against national standards and try to get accreditation for them. Alternatively, the organization might have sufficient reputation that its courses have a currency in their own right. In the UK, training by the BBC or at British Airways has enjoyed this type of reputation. As another example, in discussing an MBA designed for Flemings, the merchant bank, Bradshaw (1998b) points out that most people who leave take up positions with rival banks with whom the qualification is likely to be as useful as it is at Flemings.

It can be seen that development is not just carried out to increase the person's competence. It also serves to motivate and retain people. It benefits both the individuals and the organization. Organizations are building, motivating and retaining a resource of talented people. The individuals will be in the right state of preparation to continue to advance their careers. Hopefully, this will be with their present employer, but if the unforeseen happens, such as a merger, they have the 'insurance' of being employable elsewhere.

There is, then, something of a blurring of the distinction made by Kidd (1997) between two types of career development activity. The first focuses on the organization's needs; the second on the individual's concerns. The former includes fast-track programmes and provision of information about career ladders and paths. The latter includes career planning workshops and individual career counselling. Activities that focus on the individual's concerns are not philanthropic. They aim to benefit the organization by making people more aware of their development needs and helping people to make adult decisions about their futures. Macauley and Harding (1996) describe an example of one such workshop. It is at the UK subsidiary of SCO, a US software company. The self-development process was designed to reduce people's dependence on other people for career management. Another example is provided by Altman (1998). He describes a career development programme at Rothmans, the tobacco company. Its objective was to make people more dynamic rather than waiting for 'the call' for their next job in the company. Altman contrasts the programme run by Rothmans with one run by Sun Microsystems. In the case of Sun, people are already highly self-reliant and the aim of the programme is that 'the search for a new and satisfying job will start – and end – within the company' (p. 42).

By getting people to consider their futures, there is of course the risk that the career management programme will stimulate employees to think in the opposite way and to look outside the organization rather than within it for their next move (Wooldridge, 1998). Wills (1997) confronts the possibility of people being encouraged to leave by career management schemes, but presents the argument that the costs of this are far outweighed by the goodwill, energy and motivation that such schemes produce. Wills, like Altman, uses the example of the Manage Your Career programme at Sun Microsystems which consists of a workshop for self-analysis of participants' values and career decisions. It is followed by discussion with a manager who will act as a coach. Another example of a career management programme is provided by Holbeche (1995). She describes a centre run at a management college to which people from different organizations can come. The aims are to create a development plan, work with others and evaluate progress. She suggests the centre 'sends strong signals to employees that they are valued' (p. 27).

However, a cautionary tale is provided by Kossek *et al.* (1998). They studied a workshop run for a US employer in the transportation industry. The aim of the workshop was to get people to take greater responsibility for managing their careers. Kossek *et al.* (1998) describe the training as 'designed to change employees' attitudes to increase their level of initiation of certain behaviors associated with career self-management; informal feedback seeking on current performance and developmental needs, and preparing for internal or external job mobility' (p. 947). They found that the training actually lowered these behaviours and they conclude that 'when done as an isolated HR strategy, some career self-management training may be worse than none at all' (p. 953).

The case study provided by Kossek *et al.* introduces the need to be cautious with career self-management programmes. It is one thing to encourage people to be adaptable, self-responsible and open to feedback and to have a belief in their ability to manage their career. It is another to encourage them to look outside the organization for their next job. Obviously, considering opportunities outside the present employer is part of the package of career self-management. However, making this part of the formal programme must surely convey a message to people that the organization is fairly relaxed about whether they stay or go.

Maybe it was this relaxed attitude that caused the negative results that were observed by Kossek *et al.* One way for the organization to show that it is not relaxed but actively wants the person to manage their career internally is to follow Sun Microsystems' example and provide coaching and mentoring as a means of supporting people.

Coaching and mentoring provide a bridge between on- and off-the-job development. Personal coaching, as Hardingham (1998) observes, tends to be particularly sought by people who are senior and who have undergone a change of role, perhaps from professional/technical to managerial. They face a steep learning curve and need to acquire the attributes of success. In many ways personal coaching is a euphemism for counselling and it would seem a highly suitable intervention in the light of the qualities that the person is trying to change. These might be quite central to the person, such as their interpersonal skills or self-confidence.

Coaches might well be external experts and the focus is helping people acquire skills. Mentoring can also be seen as a form of coaching. In this case, the coach is less concerned with helping the acquisition of skills. Instead, the focus is on ensuring the person is able to make use of their skills and is not blocked by politics or a lack of knowledge of a system. Mentors tend to be internal and from the line. However, there are exceptions. Maitland (1998b) describes an annual programme run by the International Women's Forum whereby women with 'uncommon potential' get mentors outside their organizations to help them make the transition from manager to leader, helping them overcome the 'glass ceiling'.

## WHO IS RESPONSIBLE?

The mentoring described by Maitland (1998b) takes place independently of the organizations that employ the future leaders who benefit from it. This introduces the final issue of this chapter which is whether it is the organization or the individual that is responsible for development. Clearly, at some fundamental level it is the individual. Certainly there cannot be the option of development being only the organization's responsibility. It is the individual who is developing and there is obviously a responsibility on the part of the individual to take development forward.

However, there seems to have been a trend recently to extend this insight to mean it should not be the organization's responsibility at all.

As Kidd (1997) points out, many organizations have been trying to place more responsibility on the individual for development. One reason is that it encourages the flexibility demanded by the environment. However, the difficulty with a total handover is that people need help and support with their development. Maurer and Tarulli (1994) showed that employee development activity was consistently related to the perception of supportive rules, policies, guidelines and regulations. Aside from needing support, people also expect support. Indeed, Prickett (1998c) reports research by Sturges that showed a full 91 per cent of UK graduates who were surveyed expect their employer to help with development. Organizations are tending to acknowledge this. Hirsh and Jackson (1996) suggest that the pendulum might have swung back so that self-development processes are being repositioned to allow the organization and participant to 'reach a shared career development agenda' (p. 22). The approach is well represented in the Cadbury Schweppes 1997 annual report which states 'development is a shared responsibility'.

Whatever the particular development opportunities, organizations need to ensure people gain the most benefit from them. Holbeche (1998) found that of the factors that high-flyers reported as helpful to their development, the biggest was having a supportive management, with 39 per cent finding this helpful. It was closely followed by a supportive colleague, mentioned by 30 per cent. Conversely, the greatest blocks to development were also to do with people, especially an unhelpful management. She goes on to note that the importance of support from others is all the greater if people feel that 'aspects of the organisation's culture such as rivalry among peers or micropolitics prevents people from advancing in the ways they would like' (p. 42).

If support is important, it is also hard to achieve. Hirsh and Jackson (1996) describe how the HR function tends nowadays to be too small and fragmented to offer ongoing support for initiatives. They also describe problems with the follow-through to development plans, including line managers who are too busy to provide support and participants not fulfilling their development plans because of short-term business pressures. Much the same comments come from Guest and Mackenzie Davey (1996) who describe how 'many managers paid lip service to the importance of their role in the development of subordinates' but could not find the time. Just as pessimistically, Clutterbuck (1998) observes that 'in practice, "task activities" (getting the job done) almost always push aside learning activities'. He suggests the 'concept of specific recognition of people developers' to encourage managers in these activities and to help them become role models for future generations.

The general air of half-hearted support for people's development has to be tackled. It can only be changed by the directors of the organization believing in the strategy of building a resource and giving it their full support. In too many cases, the message that is conveyed is the opposite. Whenever there is a crunch point, development is a luxury that must not interfere with 'the real work'. This attitude filters down to staff and, as we have seen, can be extremely demotivating as well as courting the danger of the organization losing out in the long term to competitors who have developed their people more assiduously.

If the organization is to implement a strategy of gaining people's commitment by being committed to them, learning activities have to be a priority. The activities enable the creation of a virtuous circle. The organization has talented people properly prepared for the future. In these circumstances, there is not even the temptation to replace them. They are the right people. Without such a commitment to development, the strategy of being committed to the core seems hollow. Inevitably it will be tested when the future arrives and the core will be found ill-prepared. To avoid this and to stop short-term pressures dominating, development and learning need to be within the culture and fabric of the organization. It needs to be truly a learning organization. Rajan and van Eupen (1997) emphasize that 'leadership development needs to be firmly embedded into corporate culture' (p. 31) and Storey *et al.* (1997) make clear that development cannot be subject to fads and fashions if it is to work. It needs to be long-term. It is part of a strategic response and not a panic reaction. It is part of a culture of commitment.

# Showing you care:    13
# cultures of commitment

An emphasis on development and being a learning organization is just one piece in the jigsaw of culture that will show people that the organization is committed to them. All the other pieces have to give the same message. This coherence will only be achieved if there is an underlying attitude that values people. There needs to be a genuine attitude of partnership. In its absence, there are bound to be jarring notes. These exceptions will create doubts in people's minds about the authenticity of any claims of commitment.

In particular there are ways of treating people that will suggest commitment and ways that will cause doubt. They will have this effect because they are tell-tale signs that the value is genuine or otherwise. They are ways of treating people that people would see as following naturally if the organization really cares. At an uncontroversial level, Pfeffer (1998) includes reducing status distinctions and barriers among his practices of successful organizations. People are referred to in a language that shows they matter and offered office space or other accommodation that also indicates their value. Another practice discussed by Pfeffer is sharing information with people. He says such sharing 'makes simple, common sense' (p. 95).

These practices seem to require no debate. However, there are other ways of treating people that require more consideration. The first is the offer of security.

## OFFERING SECURITY

Pfeffer puts 'employment security' at the head of his 'sixteen practices for managing people' in his 1994 book and at the head of his 'seven practices of successful organizations' in his 1998 book. He cites the example of the Lincoln Electric Company which guarantees employees with over three years of service that they will not be laid off. Pfeffer (1994) observes that this 'signals a long-standing commitment by the organization to its work force' (p. 31).

However, it is not clear that the sort of undertaking by Lincoln and urged by Pfeffer is entirely honest. Employment cannot be guaranteed. The organization can only do its level best to preserve people's employment. It is really an attitude more than an undertaking that is needed within a strategy of gaining commitment and loyalty by treating people in an honest way and offering commitment.

The strategy of commitment recognizes that people might move to another job, just as there might be occasions when the organization has to part company with the member of staff. What matters is the organization's attitude. It should be seen to value people, to make promises it can keep and to do all it can to choose people carefully and develop them, thereby providing them with a long-term future.

The sense of security should follow from the organization having a commitment to people rather than having a 'hire them, fire them' mentality. This is different from making a straightforward pledge of security. The organization should think very carefully about the limits to the security it can deliver and make sure it does not offer guarantees that clearly cannot be honoured.

## OFFERING CARE

While the organization might not be able to guarantee security, it needs to make people feel secure. Kahn (1996) describes the paradox that people behave in a more self-reliant manner if they feel they have a secure base. If the organization actively seeks out people who are sufficiently secure to cope with change, it then needs to ensure they remain secure by offering a culture of support. Kahn (1996) calls it 'a real irony' that 'organizations that require members to create new collaborations, markets, and products in order to justify their continuing employments are those most in need of ways to enable members to feel secure' (p. 161). Without the sense of security, people will be disabled from being self-reliant. In other words, people will achieve secure employment by behaving in ways that are helped if they already have security. To some extent, their security will come from within, but it must also be fostered by the organization.

Kahn suggests that organizations need to engage in caregiving. He lists dimensions of caregiving which are concerned with giving a person the sense that they are understood, valued and supported in a consistent way. He suggests that groups are the most likely source of 'secure bases' at work and describes how organizations can foster the conditions that will promote the caregiving role of groups. These conditions include rewarding group performance and encouraging group leaders to initiate and monitor caregiving interactions.

Kahn also suggests that there is a role for career development professionals in caregiving, both in directly offering support and also in assisting groups examine 'the quantity and quality of their caregiving and care-receiving interactions' (p. 176).

Kahn is careful to point out that caregiving does not mean taking over and intruding. There is a need for a boundary that gives people a sense of autonomy while also being supported. Where the boundary is drawn varies between occupations. Caregiving is, he suggests, more common in the 'caring' professions like social work than in investment banking. It would, of course, be easy to scoff at whether caregiving is even needed for investment bankers. The answer is that it might matter less for those who are interested only in a transaction. For those people who are looking to form a commitment to the organization, a lack of a sense of caregiving will make the relationship seem somewhat empty.

## AVOIDING THE WORST

If the organization faces difficulties, the strategy of offering commitment dictates that people are laid off only as a last resort. Other possibilities should have been explored and seen to have been explored first. In particular, the directors and stockholders should take a short-term sacrifice rather than laying people off to preserve their own benefits and return from the organization. It is also important that staff see a degree of prudence in policies of expansion and hiring in 'good times'. Reckless and opportunistic expansion will be seen as just that if it is followed by the need for lay-offs. A firm that truly cares and is committed to its staff will only take new people into its core if it foresees a long-term future for them. Short-term surges in demand are best met by hiring people on temporary contracts. Commitment is neither given nor expected.

## FACING THE WORST

### Redundancies

The worst cannot always be avoided. The environment might turn impossibly hostile. A commodity-based company might see the market price drop to an unsustainable level; overseas competition using cheap labour might take away the organization's customers; turbulence in emerging markets might impact on the organization. People might have to go so that the organization can survive.

If the worst does happen and the firm has to lose people, this should be confronted in an open and honest way. Clay (1998) advises that 'helping organizations keep their lines of communication open is the key to success during organizational change', but suggests this might go against managers' instincts. Yeung and McBride (1998) comment, 'when an employee's career and livelihood are at stake, it is impossible to give too much information'. They talk later about the importance of keeping the top team's loyalty by consulting them and 'managing the departure of senior people from the company with sensitivity and generosity'.

Hopefully the same courtesy would be extended to all staff. As Pfeffer (1998) makes clear, it is important at times when redundancies become inevitable that the firm does not violate its own values and norms, such as the norm of open communication. He describes how the lay-offs at Apple were handled crudely and how this had a detrimental effect on those who remained.

## Individual lay-offs

The strategy of commitment has as a fundamental requirement that the organization avoids sacking people individually from the core. The commitment can be honoured by bringing in people who are flexible. Even if a person does not turn out to be in the group of leaders or future leaders, they can still be usefully employed. In such cases, the member of staff will need to be realistic about what they can expect in terms of increases in remuneration and what they have to give in terms of effort and engagement. There is then an undertaking of commitment by the organization in return for flexibility and realism by the members of staff. However, there will also be some people who, despite the firm's best efforts, 'can't or won't change or who are redundant because of changes in technology or business conditions' (Pfeffer, 1998, pp. 124–125). As O'Neill (1997) so aptly puts it, 'even the most caring companies need to be tough-minded commercially, and the most effective managers are those who are able to handle this paradox' (p. 13). In the event of people having to be laid off, as Pfeffer makes clear, they need to be treated fairly. In particular, they need to be treated with respect and dignity rather than marched out of the building by a security guard.

## Mergers and acquisitions

Mergers and acquisitions represent a particular unforeseen event that can suddenly question people's contracts. Whatever the level of trust and partnership that has been established, it is bound to be tested by a merger or acquisition. Just how unsettling a merger can be is evidenced in a report by Welch (1998a) on the merger of Polygram with Seagram that was discussed in Chapter 3. She describes how 'Polygram is offering a total of $40 million (£24 million) in bonuses in a bid to retain staff'.

The problems, not surprisingly, arise particularly in the acquired organization. They centre around a feeling of being unwanted, the inferior partner and undervalued. For example, Sleek (1998) describes how the merger between Daimler-Benz and Chrysler Corp. 'appeared destined for trouble' because Daimler-Benz has a sense of superiority that 'will probably irk Chrysler's top management'. Sleek says one likely outcome is that 'top talent may leave the company altogether' and describes the importance after a merger that 'executives should immediately tell key employees that they're needed'. Perhaps heeding this advice, White (1998) reported several months later an advertizing campaign by Daimler-Chrysler that 'tells nervous employees the new company values them'. Meyer and Allen (1997) also describe the importance of communication. A particular form of communication was examined by Schweiger and DeNisi (1991). They found that providing 'realistic merger previews' to staff preserved people's commitment.

## Conclusion

The overall message is that if the worst happens, trust will be permanently damaged if the organization does not behave honestly with people. It needs to maximize communication, act decisively and only terminate people's contracts if there is, demonstrably, no alternative. Certainly, it does not want to end up with the state of affairs that Corzine and Tait (1999) report applies at Amoco following its merger with British Petroleum. These journalists describe how 'the large number of share options held by top Amoco executives and their generous post-merger financial packages demanded as part of the deal have left many of its former employees disillusioned, and feeling that personal financial gain played a part in the decision to give up Amoco's independence'. It seems clear that people's trust will be lost if they feel they have been sold out, even if they have been fortunate enough to hang on to their jobs.

## FAIR SHARES

The strategy of commitment and partnership is implemented by having pay systems that seem fair. This is emphasized by Reichheld (1996). He suggests that one of its consequences is that senior executives are not paid at the top of the range. Indeed Reichheld suggests they should be paid less than average. Certainly executives who are paying themselves as much as possible in the short term might create the suspicion that others will be sacrificed before they take any pain. It also suggests that they will have limited enthusiasm for investment in people's development and other initiatives that will only pay off in the longer term. This view is supported by De Geus (1997). He draws attention to fair pay as a feature of long-standing companies. He says that everyone else will feel outsiders, not members in organizations in which a few people take disproportionate benefits. He argues that they will 'trade their time and expertise for money' but this will not inspire them 'to give their all or to feel much loyalty to the enterprise or its managers' (p. 58).

Pfeffer (1994, 1998) also deals with pay among his list of management practices. He advocates 'wage compression', so that differences between people are reduced. This extends both vertically for which he (Pfeffer, 1994) comments, 'vertical pay dispersion sends a signal that the lower-paid, lower level people matter comparatively less' (p. 52). It also extends horizontally, whereby people at a given level in the organization are paid much the same as each other. At the same time, Pfeffer (1994) argues that, generally within the company, pay should be high if only because 'higher wages send a message that the organization values its people' (p. 35). The joint effect of compression and high pay clearly cannot apply from the top down. It only works if top executive pay is set at a fairly contained level, in a way that follows Reichheld's advice.

In his 1994 book, Pfeffer also argues for incentive pay, describing it as virtually dictated by fairness and justice. However, Lado and Wilson (1994) caution that this incentive pay should be team-based rather than a system that is individually based, which they label 'competence-destroying'. Certainly, it is not obvious how individual incentive pay is reconciled with the need for pay compression. Furthermore, it seems a short step from a 'winner takes all' pay system to having a similar attitude to people's employment. Indeed, by 1998 Pfeffer seems to have altered his view. He says, 'individual incentive schemes erode teamwork and trust and set people against one another in a competition for rewards' (p. 223)

## BEING STRAIGHTFORWARD

Some organizations have cultures that are over-political and poisonous. People talk badly about each other behind their backs. Factions plot how to do each other down. If this is happening, it must inevitably be with the endorsement or collusion of top management. Indeed, it most likely comes from their example.

While it would be foolish to deny the political dimension to people in organizations, it is equally foolish to think an organization can proclaim its commitment to people while condoning or encouraging unsupportive behaviour. Kakabadse and Parker (1984) describe all behaviour in organizations as political. However, they also make clear that there is a need to recognize the difference between appropriate and inappropriate behaviour. The communication of this difference needs to come from the top of the organization and to encompass the message that people are valued.

The problem for the highly political organization is that it is not a very pleasant place to work in for the very people who have the competencies that are required for the future. Organizations all too readily describe how they require 'team playing' as a competency, while condoning the single-minded back-stabber. At the very least, this breeds cynicism. The issue is discussed by Fletcher (1996) who describes how relational skills can 'get disappeared' in a culture that rewards individual achievement and mastery. This harks back to the previous chapter's discussion of 'right stuff' thinking. It leads to an emphasis on proving oneself, fostering competitive rather than cooperative behaviour. If organizations are serious about wanting relational and cooperative competencies they will need to ensure that it is these behaviours that are rewarded.

## VALUING DIVERSITY

Aside from being similar in terms of the values-backed competency framework, the organization should value diversity. Indeed, it will need to look at diverse people to find the competencies and diversity is needed to increase the chance of success in an unknown future. Among the diverse people, there is the possibility that some will possess the right approach to unforeseen challenges. The main difficulty is ensuring that the organization is 'big enough' to house a range of people. There is a whole body of literature on organizational personality to suggest that they are not naturally so. For example, Schneider et al. (1998) examined the records on the personalities of 12 739 managers from 142 organizations and found that 'organizations are relatively homogenous with regard to the personality characteristics of their managers' (p. 467). The finding is in line with theories of organizational socialization and with Schneider's (1987) attraction–selection–attrition (ASA) model. Under the ASA model, people are attracted to a particular type of organization (attraction), which is in turn attracted by them (selection); attrition is the process whereby those who are dissimilar choose to leave, or are forced out. Schaubroeck *et al.* (1998) provide examples of personality dimensions that will affect people's compatibility with organizational characteristics. People higher in internal locus of control might be expected in jobs in which one controls the administration and execution of duties. People high in need for power might prefer organizations with performance-based rewards that help satisfy their competitiveness.

Schneider (1987) describes how the process towards homogeneity starts when the founder determines the organization's original goals and hence its structure and strategy. Forever afterwards, there is the tendency towards homogeneity with people of a particular type being attracted towards the organization and remaining with it.

Not surprisingly, the tendency towards homogeneity is particularly pronounced at the upper management level of the organization (Schneider *et al.*, 1998). It will have had the longest time to operate on this group if they are grown from within. ASA theory points out the need for organizations to fight the tendency towards a restriction in the range of the kinds of people they contain. Otherwise, they will be neither capable of adapting to changes in the environment, possibly even being unaware of such changes. Supporting the ASA phenomenon, Chatman's (1991) study of graduates joining US accounting firms show how people who fit the organization better after a year of membership also attend more firm-related social events and spend more time with a mentor.

To run against this phenomenon requires a conscious decision and a lot of effort to protect the outsider. It also requires conviction that diversity is desirable both in the long term as a way of allowing for an uncertain future and in the short term as a source of 'increased adaptability and flexibility in dealing with difficult tasks involving demands for creativity and innovation' (Schneider *et al.*, 1998, p. 468). To implement diversity, Schneider (1987) suggests increasing the pool of candidates at selection. He comments that 'haphazard recruitment and/or faith in the selection process, either self-selection or organizational selection, cannot be expected to yield the non-right types required for long-term viability' (p. 448). The purposeful introduction of different types of people, people who 'aren't "just like us"' (p. 62) is also advocated by Hamel and Prahalad (1994). For this to work, they say top management must reward unorthodoxy.

## A SENSE OF COMMUNITY

An organization needs to house diversity. However, it needs to feel like a community. De Geus raises this aspect of implementing commitment when he describes the long-standing companies he studied as being communities. A similar point is made by Bartlett and Ghoshal (1995). They say that 'an organization is fundamentally a social structure' (p. 20). They go on to describe the importance of 'creating an internal context that encourages people to act in the way they would as a member of a functional family or a disciplined sporting team' (p. 21). They describe how their case study organizations 'devote enormous effort to create a sense of shared organizational identity' or 'glue' 'as well as organizational norms that value collaboration' or 'lubricant' (p. 11). The notion of aiming for the workplace to be like a community is in tune with the priorities of Generation X, the heirs of the baby boomers. Summers (1998) reports a study by Jay Conger of the University of California's Leadership Institute that suggested this sense of community was one of their needs. It is a need that should be met automatically if an organization follows the spirit of this book and the basic overall strategy of creating partnership, trust and commitment. The next chapter turns to the other motives people might be looking to satisfy at work.

# Whatever turns you on: transactions that motivate  14

Kinsman (1998) comments that 'Bill Gates may be far from the ideal boss but when Microsoft people can say "all our best workers are volunteers" (i.e. they've made so much they don't have to work, but they do because they love it), he must be getting something right' (p. 144). The level of motivation described by Kinsman is one that all organizations would like to achieve. It is, indeed, a level they need to achieve if they are to win the talent war. However, it is not necessarily a level that should be seen as remarkable. Talented, high potential people come to the world of work already motivated. The task of their leaders is to ensure that their enthusiasm is maintained. People come to work to have their needs met. If they are frustrated, good people can always move elsewhere. However committed the organization might be, people cannot be expected to work philanthropically. They need the transaction as well as the relationship.

Making generalizations about what motivates people has tended to give way to a more individualized approach. Indeed, one of the hallmarks of the transformational leader is giving individualized concern to people. The list of motivators considered below should therefore be seen as a starting point to gaining an insight on what motivates a particular person and not as applying equally to everyone.

## A NEED FOR BALANCE BETWEEN THEIR WORK AND THEIR PRIVATE LIFE

The list might start with what is said to be a priority for Generation X, alongside the need for the workplace to be a community that was dealt with in Chapter 13. Summers (1998) reports the suggestion that Generation X people are motivated by a need for balance between their work and their private life. This sense of balance also featured quite strongly in Holbeche's (1998) survey of high-flyers. A quarter of them described balance as what success means for them. It is also borne out by research by

Sturges (reported by Maitland, 1998a) who questioned graduates just before they started to work at four major employers in the UK (British Airways, British Telecommunications; Lloyds/TSB and Nestlé). She found that graduates expressed a determination not to sacrifice their lives for their careers.

Clearly, this generalization about the need for balance does not square with stories from Wall Street and the City of London, where people are reputed to be sacrificing their private lives for the six- or seven-digit bonus. There are surely some people with little sense of balance in such circumstances. None the less, employers need to be aware that it is something that many in the present generation of talent might want, perhaps more so than their predecessors. To use Schein's (1978) terminology, lifestyle integration might be becoming an increasingly prominent 'career anchor'. On the face of it, this emphasis seems to sit unhappily with the new environment that forces people to work harder and harder in order that they might compete successfully. Certainly, employers need to avoid exacerbating the contradiction by a culture of 'presenteeism' and they should be looking for opportunities to enable people to achieve balance, for example, by granting people's requests to 'work from home'.

## A SENSE OF ADVANCEMENT

If Generation X want balance, they also want advancement. Prickett (1998c) reports that Reed Personnel Services, a UK recruitment company, found that career progression was the main reason cited for people changing jobs. It was a more important factor than salary.

The need for advancement is easily frustrated. People are sold the idea that if they develop their competencies then career growth and advancement will follow (Mohrman and Cohen, 1995). Not surprisingly, problems arise when increased competency is not accompanied by advancement, or at least not by advancement as the staff member sees it. In an interview about people completing an in-house MBA, the training and development director of the investment bank, Flemings, states, 'The key is three years down the line. Can we deliver a position that is appropriate for these people? If we don't, we deserve to lose them' (Bradshaw, 1998b).

The desire to advance appears to sit unhappily with the flattened organization. To increase the tension, it is reported that people of ability are becoming more ambitious than ever to advance. Holbeche (1998) found from her survey of high-potential staff in the UK that more than half of the group envisaged a promotion as their next career step, with this applying to 83 per cent of 25–29-year-olds. She also found that the ultimate ambition of 38 per cent of people in her survey was to achieve a high level position with nobody envisaging a horizontal career for themselves.

These ambitions seem hard to reconcile with the contemporary flat structures of organizations with their limited opportunities for conventional vertical development of careers. Holbeche comments that 'few people seem really prepared to abandon ideas of conventional career progression in favour of lateral growth' (p. 5). She found that some people had got to the top of flat structures at a relatively early age. These people then need new sources of ongoing motivation. For others, Holbeche says, the sizeable gaps between the few levels in organizations may be too great. They will be demotivated by an inability to advance. The problem is starkly clear with professional service firms. As Jackson (1998b) states it, if good people are to stay they 'need the promise of a partnership'. The problem is that 'arithmetically, the firm has to grow at a minimum rate – perhaps 15 per cent a year – to accommodate them'. One ends up in a situation where the strategy of the organization is to grow purely in order that it can retain high-potential people who need to feel they are 'going places' in an organization that is doing likewise.

However, there is a danger of overstating the difficulty. First, the ambitions might apply particularly to younger people. They are in the advancement career stage which is described by Arthur and Kram (1989) as coming between the exploratory and protection stages of a person's career. This relates to Holbeche's conclusion that the promise of rapid advancement up a pre-planned route may only be a particular concern for the young and most ambitious. She suggests that older high-flyers are indeed looking for the balance that is supposed to characterize Generation X.

For those people who are in the advancement stage, organizations can provide rapid progress to people with ability. They are able to satisfy these people's ambitions by virtue of their changing structure. As described by Bartlett and Ghoshal (1995), large global organizations are moving to a new form that is 'fundamentally different from the multidivisional organization' (p. 1). By way of illustration, they describe Asea Brown Boveri (ABB), a 215 000 employee company, with a corporate headquarters of less than 100. ABB is structured around a business/geography matrix and is a federation of 1300 'front line' companies that are separate and distinct businesses. Presumably such a structure offers considerable potential for a feeling of advancement, at least in the short term and at least for those who were at the right level in the company when the structure was introduced. The heads of each of the 1300 businesses are described as having 'evolved from their traditional role of implementers of top-down decisions to

become primary initiators of entrepreneurial action, creating and pursuing new opportunities for the company' (p. 6). Bartlett and Ghoshal say the
same organizational form applies to the 'largest global companies of
today' (p. 19) like General Electric, 3M, Toyota and Canon.

The opportunities such structures open up are, indeed, witnessed by
Holbeche's survey. She found that, since joining their present company,
most of the high-flyers she questioned had become more ambitious. The
proportion with an ambition to manage a piece of the business had
increased to a third from the quarter who endorsed it on joining the
company. The increase was because people sensed they could make things
happen in their organization. Holbeche concludes that 'it appears that the
more fluid state of many organisations is giving some people at least the
chance for greater influence and autonomy. Indeed nearly half say that
there are more opportunities' (p. 45).

Even organizations that might not have changed their structures so
drastically might have changed their attitudes. For example, Chapter 9
referred to Pickard's (1997b) description of how NatWest gives high-
potential people responsible posts at a younger age than in the past. These
people used to be blocked by messages of 'you are too young'.

At the same time, organizations also need to encourage people to be
realistic. They can do so in two ways. The first is to have honest discussions with people about the opportunities that are available. For example,
Worrall and Cooper's (1997) survey found that a preponderance of middle
and junior managers were dissatisfied with their career opportunities.
Plainly all these people cannot hope to satisfy their ambitions. A second
possible initiative is to try and meet people's needs in ways other than
advancement. Organizations need to become less driven by hierarchy and
more concerned with motivating people in their present role. This is a
change that many acknowledge as necessary but which seems yet to be
addressed and given priority. A way needs to be found of creating status
for people remaining within their existing roles. It is important that they
do not see the only way of being increasingly valued as moving upwards
to another role. It is not entirely unrealistic to urge organizations to place
more emphasis on valuing people for what they are currently doing than
stressing differences in the value that is attached to different roles. Most
radically, they should consider encouraging people to stop being obsessed
by differences in seniority and by gaining promotion. This outlook needs
to be replaced by one that thinks in terms of people doing different roles
from each other but with all roles being valid and valuable by virtue of
their existence. As van Maanan and Schein (1979) observed two decades
ago, there is 'the pervasive practice in many relatively stable organizations
of encouraging most lower and middle managerial employees to aspire to
high position within the organization despite the fact that there will be

very few positions open at these levels. Perhaps the discontent of the so-called "plateaued manager" can then be seen as a result of a socialization practice that has outlived its usefulness' (p. 213).

Changes in organizational structure help meet people's need to advance and changes in attitude aim to reduce the need in the first place. Both are genuine responses to addressing people's need for advancement. On the other hand, there are more contrived ways of trying to meet people's need to advance. In particular, the design of some organizations seems to have been 'distorted' in order to motivate people. For example, investment banks have an inordinate number of people with the title 'director' or even 'managing director'. A good example is reported by Corrigan (1998) who wrote in the *Financial Times* that Goldman Sachs appointed 160 of its staff to be 'new managing directors', reporting this as a move 'to retain key staff' after withdrawing the bank's planned flotation. Although the reasoning is understandable, this type of move sets in train a job title inflation which one can only assume will not satisfy intelligent people for very long. In particular, they need a genuine sense of achievement.

## A SENSE OF ACHIEVEMENT

Holbeche reports that 46 per cent of high-flyers said that 'success' meant knowing they have achieved, got results and so on. There are two aspects to this sense of achievement that both seem motivating. One is having the chance to deliver exceptional results. The other is to meet a difficult challenge that has major relevance to the business and in a way that is visible to senior management. Conversely, a lack of challenge was said by her survey participants to be a major factor that would encourage people to leave.

Research by Sturges of London University (reported by Maitland 1998a) on graduates at four major companies (British Airways, British Tele-communications; Lloyds/TSB and Nestlé) showed 64 per cent of graduates rated intellectual challenge as particularly important. As Sturges comments, this can be placed in contrast with the boring menial jobs that many graduates are given to start with. Why organizations do this is partly explained by Arnold and Mackenzie Davey (1992). They found that graduates had a systematically higher opinion of their competencies than did their managers. The gap was particularly evident with interpersonal skills such as communication and conflict management. The researchers link the finding to attribution theory. The graduate explains successful performance as due to themselves whereas managers tend to attribute it to luck. On the other hand, failure is explained by graduates as due to the situation, whereas managers attribute it to the graduate's lack of competency. If left unchallenged the gap will result in unmet expectations, which, in turn, risks graduates becoming demotivated and leaving. It is necessary for managers to take a risk and give graduates challenging assignments so that they can develop. Equally, it requires managers to explain carefully to graduates the reasoning behind responsibilities that are not being handed over just yet.

## A SENSE OF BEING OF VALUE AND RECOGNIZED

People like to have their hard work noticed. Visibility to senior management has already been noted as a factor that Holbeche's (1998) participants felt important if they were to feel a sense of achievement. More generally, she found that a major achievement that goes unrecognized, while disheartening for anyone, 'appears to be particularly damaging to a high flyer' (p. 38). The sense of recognition and feeling appreciated motivated almost a quarter of Holbeche's sample to stay within their organization.

Apart from recognizing particular achievements, the organization must also convey to people the value it places on them generally. One contemporary insult, as Cordon *et al.* (1998) observe, is to be considered 'non-core'. This might be inflicted on people at entry even if they are seen as potentially in the core. As insulting for the professional staff of an organization whom I interviewed recently was the label 'trainee'. These people felt the title ignored their level of qualification.

## MONEY

Money was what success meant for 14 per cent of Holbeche's sample. This is a large percentage in comparison to the mere 4 per cent who were said to be motivated by financial reward. The weakness of money as a motivator seems supported by London University's survey of graduates, as reported by Prickett (1998b).

However, despite all that such surveys say about it, companies continue to use money to try and retain people. Donkin (1998c) describes how 'many companies prefer to throw more money' at people to keep them. He describes how stock options, bonuses and other incentives are widely used in a bid to retain staff.

Obviously, money might be a short-term 'bandage' to keep people, but even for this use it needs to be borne in mind that only 20 per cent of Holbeche's sample said more money would retain them and then it was only 'for a while' (p. 61). Clearly, the power of money will depend on the amount and on how long 'a while' is. Littlefield (1997) describes how

Unisys has developed a 'radical new pay formula in an effort to cut turnover' among programmers. People can either join on a contract giving normal pay and benefits or forgo the benefits and, after three years, receive a bonus of between 50 and 120 per cent of the first year's salary, depending on their specialism.

## FLEXIBLE BENEFITS

If money itself is not a powerful motivator, one might think the same applies to proxies for money. Not so, according to Duggal's (1998) report of a survey by Arthur Andersen. It suggested 'employers must provide incentives if they are to hold on to talented, exceptional, effective employees'. Within the realm of flexible benefits are included company cars, pension schemes, medical insurance and buying additional days off as well as vouchers and discounts and child care and leisure activities. The survey suggests that only 10 per cent of firms in the UK have flexible benefits and Duggal reports that nearly all those who have introduced it believe that Flex has met their objectives, 'particularly as a tool to aid staff retention and recruitment'.

## A SENSE OF AUTONOMY

Hunt (1998a) describes his experience with members of Generation X at London Business School. He observes that those born in the 1950s and 1960s were a 'new breed of high-flyers' who prized autonomy and controlling their careers. The desire for autonomy, Hunt says, was diminished by recession, but nowadays, once again he finds hard evidence of it in his students. For the more extreme of Hunt's students the answer might be to act as consultants rather than members of an organization. Maybe, they are avoidant in terms of their attachment to organizations. For the remainder, tolerance of organizations will be easier if they are given space. It is a need that overlaps with wanting to be trusted. Kidd and Smewing (1997) report a greater commitment in people who felt trusted, respected and given authority by their line managers. In other words, these people felt empowered.

Autonomy can refer to teams as well as individuals. Janz et al. (1997) looked at a team's autonomy with regard to decisions over four aspects of work. These were the product, planning, people and the work process. The results showed that the motivation of team members was positively associated with autonomy for decisions concerning people, whatever the interdependence of team members. On the other hand, motivation was associated positively with autonomy for planning and for products only under conditions of low interdependence. Low interdependence can, of course, itself be seen as a form of autonomy. Those with a high need for autonomy might need to be autonomous individuals rather than autonomous within a team. Organizations face dilemmas in granting people such high degrees of autonomy. Not only does it go against the team ethos, but it can also enable 'rogue' behaviour such as that seen in the Leeson affair where an autonomous trader bankrupted a bank. Yet, organizations need precisely this high level of autonomy in people who are to run a division or subsidiary. It is almost a prerequisite. The organization needs a high degree of sophistication if it is to manage such people. It is a sophistication that is often missing, as witnessed in a number of high profile resignations. For example, a lack of a sense of being trusted is said to have been the cause of the resignation of Carter McClelland, reported as one of the highest flyers in Deutsche Bank (Lewis and Harris, 1998). He was heading the Bank's American operations, but repeatedly found his plans 'scuppered by Frankfurt-based Deutsche executives'.

Just six weeks later the *Financial Times* carried a similar story, this time featuring the two joint heads of corporate finance at Barings who left after a row with their parent company, ING. The story (Martinson, 1998) describes how the two objected 'to ING's plans for their department. They are understood to have wanted to maintain the high level of independence enjoyed by the business since ING bought Barings.' Not long after, the *Financial Times* carried a report by Harris (1998) that 'the chief executive of ING Barings has quit after only five months following a disagreement over European strategy with the UK-based investment bank's Dutch owner'.

In similar vein, the *Wall Street Journal* reported (Lipin, 1998) how the head of investment banking at Lazard Frères on Wall Street had resigned, having had a request to make a particular investment rejected by the chairman and CEO. Outside the finance sector, Blackwell (1998) reported in the *Financial Times* the resignation of Richard Furse, the CEO of Ronson, whose appointment had been 'confirmed only in March'. Blackwell writes, 'it is understood that Mr Furse felt it impossible to manage the group because of interference from board members'. There seems to be a real tension between the need to control that parent companies feel and need for autonomy that individual executives have. Companies appear to be putting their executives in a very difficult position. Presumably, the ability to formulate strategies and take independent decisions is part of the job description, but then the parent does not seem willing to delegate fully to these people. It wants to lean over their shoulder. Either this tendency needs to change or the parent companies should appoint people with less need for autonomy, and accept the consequences.

## EACH TO THEIR OWN

Thus far, the discussion has been of what motivates high-potential people, generally. However, as the introduction to the chapter made clear, individual differences need to be taken into account. One way of doing so has been presented by Sturges (1998). She surveyed 36 managers in a UK telecommunications company, their number being evenly divided between men and women. She identified three dimensions of motivation, namely:

1. **Internal**  This covered criteria concerning:

   (a)  Achievement. A sense of achievement and personal development;

   (b)  Accomplishment. Feeling one was good at one's job;

   (c)  Enjoyment. Interest and enjoyment from work;

   (d)  Integrity. Including feeling work is worth while;

   (e)  Balance. Between work and home life.

2. **External intangible**  This covered the criteria of:

   (a)  Personal recognition. Being respected and being the expert;

   (b)  Influence. Leaving one's mark on the organization.

3. **External**  These included the criteria of:

   (a)  Grade;

   (b)  Reward, especially pay.

Sturges categorized her sample into four:

- **Climbers**  People mainly motivated by external criteria
- **Experts**  Mainly motivated by internal accomplishment and intangible personal recognition
- **Influencers**  The external intangible of influence
- **Self-realizers**  Achievement and balance

Sturges found that demographically men and younger people were more likely to use external criteria. Thus, all the climbers were men and relatively young, a finding that fits well with the earlier discussion on the need for advancement. Sturges also found that the experts and self-realizers were mainly women. Influencers were evenly divided between men and women, but were generally older.

The work by Sturges provides a guide to how people might differ from each other in their motives. Ideally, organizations would use findings such as these and then find out precisely what each individual is looking for. Holbeche (1998) advises that 'human resource managers should have a conversation with each of the high flyers in their organisation to find out what really motivates them and see to what extent their needs can be accommodated' (p. 79). By having such a conversation, the organization can ensure it puts together a transaction that motivates the individual and acts, with the relationship on offer, to retain them. Such conversations are an integral part of career management.

# Managing careers for commitment 15

Career management and succession planning are mirror images of each other. The individual has a career that is managed and the organization has a succession plan. The strategy of showing a commitment to the core should be nowhere better revealed than in the organization's approach to career management and succession planning. If the strategy is followed, career management should be used to show individuals that the organization is taking a long-term perspective with them. It should be designed to ensure their dévelopment and it should be aimed at addressing their motives. The organization should receive its pay-off from the strategy by being able to carry out succession planning with greater hope that the successors will still be there when the time comes to succeed.

## ORGANIZATION MANAGED

One way of implementing career management is for the organization to take the lead. People are moved and given career opportunities at the behest of a 'chess master' who has an oversight of people in the core. Certainly this is the way that career management generally was conducted in the past. However, the approach is paternalistic. Organizations nowadays want people to take responsibility for their own development and not to leave it as a problem for their employer. Furthermore, people with the overall sense of self-responsibility that is needed by organizations will themselves want to examine the choices and make decisions for themselves.

A particular problem with the organization-managed approach is that it very easily slips from being paternalistic and benevolent into a form of destruction testing. McCall (1998) describes how organizations can, all too readily, fall into the trap of leading people into situations to see if they sink or swim rather than systematically developing them. He sees the approach as the trap of 'right stuff' thinking. The premise is that the organization has found people with abilities and then needs to set about strengthening them in a Darwinian 'survival of the fittest'. McCall describes how the organization can contribute to derailments under the survival of the fittest model. He provides a case study to illustrate the organization's contribution. The case study was a multibillion dollar, US-based, multinational in which 'high potential managers were moved rapidly and typically within narrow functional channels or business unit silos. When they inevitably hit a situation requiring dramatically new or different skills and their performance subsequently declined, the unforgiving, performance driven culture emerged and derailed them' (p. 55).

The destruction-testing approach seems to be almost an underhand dreaming up of traps, which unbeknown to the member of staff are being used as tests. A much more healthy approach is for the organization and member of staff jointly to review what experiences will be valuable and beneficial for development. The role for the organization is to help ensure that staff with high potential are provided with the experiences needed for their development. It should then review the outcomes of these experiences with each of them.

The member of staff would still be confronted with challenging experiences. Indeed earlier chapters made clear that people both enjoyed and found developmental such experiences. However, they need to be provided and reviewed openly. Otherwise people will see themselves as led into a trap and the organization will destroy talented people who might not meet the final test but were perfectly good up to that point.

The 'chess master' approach to career management, then, seems inappropriate to today's circumstances whether it is paternalistic or more devious. One alternative is for the organization to aim for more of a partnership with staff, entering into a dialogue about people's careers and what experiences will be developmental. However, some organizations have gone further and largely abandoned their own role, leaving people to self-manage their careers.

## SELF-MANAGED CAREERS

Just as development is ultimately the responsibility of the person developing, so too a career belongs fundamentally to a person. No one else decides whether or not to accept an employer or whether or not to leave them. This is a truism, but it is a very different matter to extend it to its logical conclusion. The self-managed approach is a hands-off approach. It questions whether there is any need for the organization to get involved in career management. The hands-off approach clearly overlaps with treating people as temporary. It seems part of the package of the boundaryless career.

However, it is possible to argue that even organizations that are committed to people should leave them to self-manage their careers. One argument for self-managed careers is that it gets people away from thinking that the organization will look after them without they themselves having to take responsibility. It also seems well suited to the world of chaos. Individuals might be seen as best placed to pick the opportunities of greatest interest to them from those that are available at any time. If the future is unknown, arguably it is more honest to leave it to individuals to make their own choices.

Hall and Mirvis (1995) argue strongly for the 'protean career', which is one that the person manages to meet their needs. They say that we should 'consider seriously the idea that an organization should not be in the business of career planning' (p. 335). Instead, the organization acts as a facilitator. They suggest it is 'incumbent on firms to ensure that employees are exposed to a variety of challenging work assignments, develop both short-term performance-related skills and the meta-skills needed for long-term adaptability, and have the freedom and support to self-design their careers in line with the contours of a changing organization' (p. 335). Mayo (1991) describes how it is a common approach to leave decisions about career direction to the individual, while providing information and resources to help the decision.

In many respects, this sounds fine and, certainly, self-management seems a popular option with employers. A survey by the consultants Blessing/White, reported by Coyle (1998), suggests that 50 per cent of US firms and 42 per cent in the UK do not provide careers advice. However, the logic of some of the firms in the survey is that career management opens the door for staff to leave. This seems bizarre logic and introduces the problem with self-management. Strictly speaking, it makes no distinctions between people. The organization provides all employees with opportunities. It is left to staff to take advantage of them. The organization seems in danger of forgetting the very reason it brings in high potential people. It is to develop and realize that potential. As Holbeche says, 'succession planning has long been seen as an organisationally owned process aimed at securing the organisation's future' (p. 76). Nowadays what should have changed is not the aim, but the exclusivity of the ownership. In other words, as Wooldridge (1998) puts it, 'the need for organisations to undertake career management and development initiatives is as compelling as ever. What has changed from the traditional career management strategy is the context. Today, the forward looking organisation needs to respect the fact that the employee is in the driving seat, responsible for their own development.'

If the organization does not participate in the management of people's careers, it is quite possible that it will lose the people it would like to keep, while many of the people who remain are nursing an illusion. They will end up dissatisfied and feeling duped. Hall and Fukami (1979) say they would 'question the value (indeed, the ethics) of the current wave of career planning programs' (p. 154) that rely solely on the individual. They say, 'The implicit assumption seems to be that once the person identifies a career plan, he or she will be able to implement it' (p. 154).

The complexities and difficulties are described by Kossek *et al.* (1998). They say that people who have been exposed to the techniques of self-management such as networking and seeking informal feedback and career advice will find it difficult to implement them unless the context is favourable. The value of the techniques needs to be recognized by the culture.

However, even if the culture is favourable, it seems far better for the organization to take an interest and reach a shared view with staff on career possibilities and appropriate developmental experiences. Gaining these experiences requires negotiation with managers, a process that is far more likely to work successfully if the organization is working in partnership with the individual. Certainly, the complexities of gaining experiences argue against pure self-management of careers.

It does not seem good enough for organizations to reason that the future is so uncertain that it is best left to the individual alone to make choices. The organization has at least as good a view of the future as the individual, and arguably a better one. It must also be the case that the *management* of an internal career will be far more effective if the organization and individual are in partnership rather than it being left entirely to the individual. Above all the partnership approach conveys the organization's commitment to the person's future within the organization.

## PARTNERSHIP MANAGED

Recognition of the need for the organization to be involved is reflected in the case study of Cable and Wireless, as described by Altman (1998). The company apparently started out in 1994 with a career *action* centre, for which 'personal initiative was the major theme' (p. 45). Subsequently, it was recognized that both the individual and the company have a role in managing careers and even the name of the centre was changed to career *management* centre to reflect this recognition. The centre now provided by Cable and Wireless is an example of how career management can be seen as ultimately in the hands of the individual but needing the organization's support and involvement.

Some, particularly large organizations, have consistently maintained an active part in career management and succession planning throughout the era of self-management. They continued to have graduate entry schemes and high-flyer cadres. For example the *IPD guide on international management development* describes how Unilever aims to:

- Ensure a flow of high-quality management which is sufficient to meet the company's overall growth plan

- Ensure fully effective top level succession planning

- Provide an essential part of the company's 'glue'

However, the approach of organizations like Unilever is less paternalistic than in the past and is best described as a partnership approach to career management. As Hirsh and Jackson (1996) say, succession planning 'has had to adapt to changing times' (p. 22). Rather than expecting the individual to go wherever the organization wants, succession planning has to take greater account of the individual's aspirations and preferences.

Working as a partnership recognizes that it is the empowered person who owns the career. The partnership also encourages the quality the organization needs most – namely people's adaptability. The person has to be self-responsible. However, the partnership also enables the organization to contribute and to play its part in the management of people's careers.

In the partnership approach, the line manager clearly has a crucial role and it is one for which training is needed so that a consistent and accurate message is given by different managers on career possibilities. In this, they will need support from the HR function. Holbeche (1998) provides an example of such training to ensure the success of the partnership in action. She describes an organization that trains its executives to carry out career counselling. Each of them has a number of 'clients' from the ranks of the high-flyers. She says that the objective 'is not to promise rapid progression up the hierarchy but to convey the message that the organisation values these individuals and is interested in their development. Being open with these individuals has not proved a problem, quite the reverse' (p. 77).

This introduces the importance of honesty in the partnership approach. It is important that both sides communicate what they want and are able to offer in return. This will help avoid staff maintaining unrealistic career aspirations that are bound to end with a sense of frustration. It will also enable the organization to do its best to find a way of responding to people's needs, for example, by giving them additional responsibilities or arranging a secondment. The aim should be to face up to reality but also to adapt reality. Holbeche concludes that the overall effect of being open and honest is that it 'may allow for more detailed, realistic career planning and lead to better retention' (p. 77).

The partnership approach to career management is less prescriptive and deterministic about each individual than the approach that was led by organizations and this is mirrored in contemporary succession planning. Succession planning used to be essentially a matter of finding names to replace the people currently filling slots on the organization chart. Career management would be about moving people to a state of readiness to succeed. However, organizations nowadays are not sufficiently clear on their future structure and needs for so mechanistic a process of succession planning to be appropriate. As Hall and Mirvis (1995) comment, 'there is simply too much uncertainty about future organizational needs to chart out prospective career paths and steer people through precise develop-mental sequences' (p. 335). An additional drawback to the structured approach was that being a successor was a basis for complacency for the chosen person and frustration for the rest.

To get past the rigidities of a model of succession planning based upon the assumed certainties of the past, organizations can think in terms of having a high-potential cadre or a talent club. Holbeche (1998) describes these as being made up of people 'who are being developed to fill positions at a given level in the organisation' (p. 75). She reports how this approach has been adopted by British Airways and she also describes how the Dow Chemical Company uses competencies for global leadership to determine who is in the 'ready now' group. McCall also reports that 'some companies have created "high potential" pools to identify talent and to provide those so identified with special developmental attention ... the people whose careers fall under this control are considered to be "corpo-rate property"' (p. 142). The aim, then, is to plan for pools of people who can fulfil roles. It is done through the organization knowing the sort of people they need for the role, choosing and developing them.

Providing career moves that will enable the person to develop is, however, easier said than done. McCall entitles a chapter in his book 'Who gets what job: the heart of development'. As McCall puts it, the dilemma that the organization faces is whether to offer a particular post to the person most suited to it now or the person who will gain most from it developmentally. He suggests that 'of course, for some key positions and at certain critical times it would be a mistake to consider anyone but the most qualified candidate ... Many succession possibilities leave room for calculated risk, however, and here is where having 'B list' candidates – people who could *learn* the most if they had an opportunity to tackle the assignment – can improve the developmental outcomes of succession decisions significantly (p. 146).

However, he notes that this risk-taking for development is not encouraged by the reward systems of many organizations. They are structured for short-term performance and under these circumstances filling a position with someone who is developing can affect the financial results and hence the bonus of the person managing the post. This clearly discourages managers from taking on people who need to achieve developmental objectives. A similar point is made by Holbeche (1998). She notes that 'senior management attention is usually focused on financial and technological matters or concerned with market share' (p. 69).

To make the system run in favour of development McCall advocates changing the reward system so that, at least, people are not punished, and are maybe even rewarded, for developing others. He cites General Electric as an exemplary organization for encouraging the movement of people across boundaries to bring about their development. It does so by the executive resources staff providing managers with a list of candidates from across the organization when they have a vacancy to fill.

The General Electric example illustrates that some central input to career management is needed. However, as Holbeche notes, the problem in many organizations is that the HR department has been greatly reduced in size and its responsibilities have been 'devolved to the line, leaving no-one to take overall responsibility for managing the organisation's succession needs. In decentralised organisations, this becomes particularly marked with each region looking after its own staffing requirement' (p. 11). She describes the dilemma of 'how to identify and develop "high potential" employees in different regions without harming the autonomy of regional management' (p. 75).

These considerations suggest that there has to be some central management of people who are a central resource, just as the strategy of commitment has to be promoted from the centre. This means that regional autonomy has to suffer a diminution. For both the strategy and provision of career opportunities, people in decentralized structures are too focused on the short-term and immediate results to make the necessary sacrifices. The solution might involve having a central career manager or a committee of interested parties. Hirsh and Jackson (1996) note that as corporate centres have lost power to impose job moves, there has been 'rapid spread of succession or development forums' (p. 22) to gain line manager buy-in to decisions about the careers of staff.

## INDIVIDUAL OPPORTUNITY

The partnership approach aims to develop the individual's career in a way that will work for both the individual and the organization. Both sides need to think realistically but also creatively. Lawler (1994) describes the competence-based organization as one in which there are multiple career tracks. One possible track is to become a greater and greater expert in an area. On the other hand, a managerial career track 'might involve the acquisition of a broad understanding of how the organization operates and training in various types of managerial activities' (p. 12).

People need to be encouraged to decide which track they are on and this can be facilitated at a career planning workshop. This might be based around an instrument such as Schein's (1978) Career Anchors which helps people to think about their own priorities. The organization needs to be honest and open with people about their prospects if they do not follow a managerial/leadership track. It must decide whether it requires senior people who are professional experts rather than leaders. If it does have the requirement for professional experts, it must also provide these people with their own career track. If the requirement is not there, the organization must make this clear to people at the outset when people are recruited. If the consequence is that there are recruitment problems, the organization might have to rethink its career tracks and create an opportunity for professionals to advance through the system.

Large organizations have different managerial career tracks quite apart from the non-managerial tracks. Uniliver's approach is described by the *IPD guide on international management development* (1997). Graduates are offered three career options:

- A vertical career within a company or product group

- A diversified career, moving across product groups

- An international career, moving between countries

In providing experiences and movement, the organization must decide whether it should be deliberately fast-tracking its high-potential staff. Certainly, fast-tracking appears to have become fashionable again in the later 1990s, a major reason being to motivate people. The possibility of rapid advancement is clearly a major selling point to recruits. Equally, it can be demotivating to people not on the fast track. To try to counteract the demotivating effects, organizations usually provide these people with a way to join the fast track by demonstrating that they have the necessary potential. By definition, few people will succeed in making the transition and the many people who do not do so need to have the importance of their present roles emphasized. The fast track needs to be presented as less of a golden prize than it is in some organizations. Preferably, its benefits in terms of rapid development and responsibility need to be available in a less divisive package. In particular, the opportunity to move ahead rapidly should be available without elevating a few people to a formal fast track.

Of course, there will always be a limit to these opportunities. Everyone cannot move ahead rapidly and there are limits to what 'ahead' means. If roles are occupied, the only possibility comes with growth of the organization. There cannot be a magic answer to this. Expecting magic is the stuff of children and returns the organization to the role of a parent. If the organization faces the problem of ambitious and able people who are blocked, it needs to have an honest discussion with them and try to find a way forward that will meet their needs. It can also try and not let the situation recur. It needs to be clear about just how many high-potential people it should recruit for eventual leadership roles. In addition, talented people who are recruited for their professional work should be able to assume the full responsibilities for that work as soon as they are ready. Organizing such people into a hierarchy with status differences inevitably means the work of the group has to be divided so that people at each level do not do the work done by people at the level below them. The benefits of this system need to be weighed against the costs in terms of introducing unnecessary blocks and frustrations. Everyone wants to move to the next status level, but people cannot move ahead when they are ready. If everyone moved up, there would be nobody to do the work at the bottom. 'Junior' people therefore leave in order to develop and gain responsibility. One alternative might be to share out this work if it needs talented people to do it. There will still be leaders of talented teams and even leaders of leaders. Their skill is to treat the people who work for them as individuals and give them responsibility when they are ready. They need, in short, to adopt a partnership approach.

# Bibliography

Agnew, Christopher R., Van Lange, Paul A. M., Rusbult, Caryl E. and Langston, Christopher A. (1998) Cognitive interdependence: Commitment and the mental representation of close relationships. *Journal of Personality and Social Psychology*, **74**, No. 4, 939–954.

Altman, Barbara W. and Post, James E. (1996) Beyond the 'social contract': An analysis of the executive view at twenty-five large companies. Chapter 2 in Douglas T. Hall and Associates. *The career is dead – Long live the career: A relational approach to careers*. San Francisco: Jossey-Bass.

Altman, Yochanan (1998) The big match. *People Management*, 26 November, 42–45.

Anderson, Neil and Ostroff, Cheri (1997) Selection as socialization. Chapter 20 in Neil Anderson and Peter Herriot, (Eds.) *International handbook of selection and assessment*. Chichester: John Wiley & Sons.

Antonacopoulou, Elena P. and FitzGerald, Louise (1996) Reframing competency in management development. *Human Resource Management Journal*, **6**, No. 1, 27–48.

Arkin, Anat. (1999) Campus Mentis. *People Management*, 28 January, 38–44.

Armstrong-Stassen, Marjorie (1998) The effect of gender and organizational level on how survivors appraise and cope with organizational downsizing. *Journal of Applied Behavioral Science*, **34**, No. 2, June, 125–142.

Arnold, John and Mackenzie Davey, Kate (1992) Self-ratings and supervisor ratings of graduate employees' competences during early career. *Journal of Occupational and Organizational Psychology*, **65**, Part 3, 235–250.

Arthur, Michael B. and Kram, K. E. (1989) Reciprocity at work: The separate, yet inseparable possibilities for individual and organizational development. In M. B. Arthur, D. T. Hall and B. S. Lawrence (Eds.) *Handbook of career theory*. Cambridge University Press.

Arthur, Michael B. and Rousseau, Denise M. (1996) Introduction: The boundary-less career as a new employment principle. Chapter 1 in Michael B. Arthur and Denise M. Rousseau (Eds.) *The boundaryless career*. New York: Oxford University Press.

Authers, John (1998) Making friends at the top. *Financial Times*, 20 April.

Baker, Gerard (1998) Clinton fails to win over the doubters. *Financial Times*, 20 April.

Ballantyne, Iain and Povah, Nigel (1995) *Assessment and development centres*. Aldershot, England: Gower.

Bartholomew, Kim and Horowitz, Leonard M. (1991) Attachment styles among young adults: A test of a four-category model. *Journal of Personality and Social Psychology*, **61**, No. 2, 226–244.

Bartlett, Christopher A. and Ghoshal, Sumantra. (1995) Beyond the M-form: Toward a managerial theory of the firm. http://www.gsia.cmu.edu/bosch/bart.html

Bass, B. M. and Avolio, B. J. (1990) Developing transformational leadership: 1992 and beyond. *Journal of European Industrial Training*, **14**, No. 5, 21–27.

Bayliss, Valerie (1998) Redefining work. *Royal Society of Arts Journal*, No. 2, 13–17.

Berry, Kate (1999) Fund chiefs are said to drive mergers. *Wall Street Journal*, 23 February.

Blackwell, David (1998) Kiam steps up as Ronson directors leave. *Financial Times*, 8 July.

Bowlby, John (1973) *Attachment and loss*: **2.** *Separation: Anxiety and anger*. New York: Basic Books.

Bracken, David D., Dalton, Maxine A., Jako, Robert A., McCauley, Cynthia D. and Pollman, Victoria A. (1997) *Should 360-degree feedback be used only for developmental purposes?* Greensboro, N. C.: Center for Creative Leadership.

Bradshaw, Della (1998a) For managers too successful to do an MBA. *Financial Times*, 16 February.

Bradshaw, Della (1998b) Flemings goes it alone. *Financial Times*, 14 April.

Bradshaw, Della (1998c) Stepping into clients' shoes. *Financial Times*, 20 April.

Brake, Terence (1997) Global leadership begins with strategic competency development. *Competency*, **4**, No. 3, Spring, 28–31.

Bridges, William (1997) *Creating You & Co*. London: Nicholas Brealey Publishing.

Bridges, William (1998) Redefining work. *Royal Society of Arts Journal*, No. 1, 50–55.

Brockner, Joel, Wiesenfeld, Batia M., Reed, Thomas, Grover, Steven and Martin, Christopher (1993) Interactive effect of job content and context on the reactions of layoff survivors. *Journal of Personality and Social Psychology*, **64**, No. 2, 187–197.

Buckley, M. Ronald, Fedor, Donald B., Veres, John G., Wiese, Danielle S. and Carraher, Shawn M. (1998) Investigating newcomer expectations and job-related outcomes. *Journal of Applied Psychology*, **83**, No. 3, 452–461.

Burke, Katherine (1997) Staff given formula to protect careers. *Personnel Today*, 3 July, 2.

Cascio, Wayne F. (1998) On managing a virtual workplace. *The Occupational Psychologist*, No. 35, August, 5–11.

Chatman, Jennifer A. (1991) Matching people and organizations: Selection and socialization in public accounting firms. *Administrative Science Quarterly*, **36**, 459–484.

Church, Allan H. and Waclawski, Janine (1998) The relationship between individual personality orientation and executive leadership behaviour. *Journal of Occupational and Organizational Psychology*, **71**, Part 2, June, 99–125.

Clarke, Martin (1998) Peripheral vision. *People Management*, 9 July, 47–48.

Clay, Rebecca A. (1998) Downsizing backfires on corporate America. *American Psychological Association Monitor*, January, 24.

Clutterbuck, David (1998) Fete developers. *People Management*, **4**, No. 21, 29 October, 37.

Conference Board (1997) Implementing the new employment contract: *HR Executive Review*. **4**, No. 4.

Conger, Jay (1998) Learner-leaders. *People Management*, **4**, No. 21, 29 October, 35.

Cooper, Cary (1997) The implications of the new work Millennium. *Selection and Development Review*, **13**, No. 6, December, 9–12.

Cooper, Cary (1998) The psychological implication of the changing patterns of work. *Royal Society of Arts Journal*, No. 1, 74–80.

Cordon, Carlos, Vollmann, Tom and Heikkilä, Jussi (1998) Thinking clearly about outsourcing. Mastering Global Business Supplement Part IV. *Financial Times*.

Corrigan, Tracy (1998) Goldman appoints 160 directors. *Financial Times*, 30 September.

Corzine, Robert and Tait, Nikki. (1999) Former Amoco executive quits merged group. *Financial Times*, 13 February.

Coulson-Thomas, Colin (1997) The future is virtually here. *Business Consultancy*, November, 32–33.

Coyle, Martin (1998) Report on Blessing/White survey. *Management Consultancy*, November, 4.

Currie, Leslie (1998) Managing international assignments – trends and issue. Paper presented to IPD International Forum Networking Meeting, London, 6 February.

Dauphinais, G. W. and Price, Colin. (Eds.) (1998) *Straight from the CEO: The world's top business leaders reveal ideas that every manager can use*. London: Nicholas Brealey Publishing.

Davies, Michaela, Stankov, Lazar and Roberts, Richard D. (1998) Emotional intelligence: In search of an elusive construct. *Journal of Personality and Social Psychology*, **75**, No. 4, October, 989–1015.

Davis, Donald D. (1995) Form, function, and strategy in boundaryless organizations. In Ann Howard (Ed.) *The changing nature of work*. San Francisco: Jossey-Bass.

DeFillippi, Robert J. and Arthur, Michael B. (1996) Boundaryless contexts and careers: A competency-based perspective. Chapter 7 in Michael B Arthur and Denise M Rousseau (Eds.) *The boundaryless career*. New York: Oxford University Press.

De Geus, Arie. (1997) The living company. *Harvard Business Review*, March–April, 51–59.

Donkin, Richard (1995) Careers on and off the rails. *Financial Times*, 20 December.

Donkin, Richard (1997a) Value and rewards of brainpower. *Financial Times*, 11 June.

Donkin, Richard (1997b) Plan now to avoid failed appointment. *Financial Times*, 5 November.

Donkin, Richard (1997c) When the desk becomes redundant. *Financial Times*, 26 November.

Donkin, Richard (1998a) A search for talent within. *Financial Times*, 4 March.

Donkin, Richard (1998b) Learning through doing dominates. *Financial Times*, 20 April.

Donkin, Richard (1998c) Price of downsizing. *Financial Times*, 10 June.

Donkin, Richard (1998d) Doing the knowledge. *Financial Times*, 15 July.

Donkin, Richard (1998e) Wanted: Superman. *Financial Times*, 11 November.

Donkin, Richard (1998f) Fighting the talent war. *Financial Times*, 25 November.

Driver, M. (1982) Career components: A new approach to career research. In R. Katz (Ed.) *Career issues in human resource management.* Englewood Cliffs, NJ: Prentice-Hall.

Drucker, Peter F. (1992) The new society of organizations. *Harvard Business Review*, September–October.

Duggal, Cosima (1998) Flexible policy pays benefits for employers. *Management Consultancy*, February, 17.

Dulewicz, Victor (1989) Assessment centres as the route to competence. *Personnel Management*, **21**, No. 11, November, 56–59.

Eggers, John H. (1995) Developing entrepreneurs: Skills for the 'wanna be,' 'gonna be,' and 'gotta be better' employees. Chapter 8 in Manuel London (Ed.) *Employees, careers, and job creation: Developing growth-oriented human resource strategies and programs.* San Francisco: Jossey-Bass Publishers.

Emery, F. E. and Trist, E. L. (1965) The causal texture of organizational environments. *Human Relations*, **18**, 21–32.

Ezzamel, Mahmoud, Lilley, Simon, Wilkinson, Adrian and Willmott, Hugh (1996) Practices and practicalities in human resource management. *Human Resource Management Journal*, **6**, No. 1, 63–80.

Feeney, J. A. and Noller, P. (1996) *Adult attachment.* Thousand Oaks, Calif.: Sage.

Fletcher, Joyce K. (1996) A relational approach to the protean worker. Chapter 4 in Douglas T. Hall and Associates. *The career is dead – Long live the career: A relational approach to careers.* San Francisco: Jossey-Bass Publishers.

Foster, Steve. (1998) The last competitive advantage? *Business Consultancy*, July, 11–15.

Gaertner, K. N. and Nollen, S. D. (1989) Career experiences, perceptions of employee practices, and psychological commitment to the organization. *Human Relations*, **42**, 975–991.

Ghoshal, Sumantra and Bartlett, Christopher A. (1998) Play the right card to get the aces in the pack. *Financial Times*, 28 July.

Ghoshal, Sumantra and Caulkin, Simon (1998) An escape route from ruthlessness. *Financial Times*, 18 November.

Goleman, Daniel (1998) *Working with emotional intelligence*. London: Bloomsbury Publishing.

Goyder, Mark (1998) Living tomorrow's company. *Royal Society of Arts Journal*, No. 2, 116–117.

Gratton, Lynda (1997) Tomorrow people. *People Management*, 24 July, 22–27.

Green, Richard (1998) United status. *People Management*, 11 June, 44–46.

Griffith, Victoria. (1998a) When the boss is chief scout. *Financial Times*, 23 March.

Griffith, Victoria (1998b) As close as a group can get to global. *Financial Times*, 7 April.

Guest, David and Conway, Neil (1996) *The state of the psychological contract in employment*. Issues in People Management No. 16. Institute of Personnel and Development.

Guest, David and Conway, Neil (1997) *Employee motivation and the psychological contract*. Issues in People Management No. 21. Institute of Personnel and Development.

Guest, David and Mackenzie Davey, Kate (1996) Don't write off the traditional career. *People Management*, 22 February, 22–25.

Guest, David, Mackenzie Davey, Kate and Smewing, Christopher (1998) Innovative employment contracts: A flexible friend? British Psychological Society Occupational Psychology Conference, 6–8 January, *Book of Proceedings*. Leicester, England: British Psychological Society, pp. 191–196.

Hall, Douglas T. (1996) Long live the career. In Douglas T. Hall and Associates. *The career is dead – Long live the career: A relational approach to careers*. San Francisco: Jossey-Bass Publishers.

Hall, Douglas T. and Associates (1996) *The career is dead – Long live the career: A relational approach to careers*. San Francisco: Jossey-Bass Publishers.

Hall, Douglas T. and Fukami, Cynthia V. (1979) Organization design and adult learning. In Barry M. Staw (Ed.) *Research in organizational behavior*. 1, pp. 125–167, Greenwich, Conn.: JAI Press, Inc.

Hall, Douglas T. and Mirvis, Philip H. (1995) Careers as lifelong learning. In Ann Howard (Ed.) *The changing nature of work*. San Francisco: Jossey-Bass Publishers.

Hamel, Gary and Prahalad, C. K. (1994) *Competing for the future*. Boston: Harvard Business School Press.

Handy, Charles (1991) *The age of unreason*. 2nd edition. London: Arrow Books Limited.

Handy, Charles (1996) What's it all for? Reinventing capitalism for the next century. *Royal Society of Arts Journal*, December, 33–39.

Hardingham, Alison (1998) Moments of clarity. *People Management*, 16 April, 31.

Harris, Clay (1998) Barings chief quits over new European strategy. *Financial Times*, 30 May.

Hendry, Chris and Pettigrew, Andrew (1995) Human resource management: an agenda for the 1990s. *International Journal of Human Resource Management*, **1**, No. 1, 17–43.

Heron, Michael (1998) How adults will keep up with change. *Royal Society of Arts Journal*, No. 1, 6–10.

Herriot, Peter and Anderson, Neil (1997) Selecting for change: How will personnel and selection psychology survive? Chapter 1 in Neil Anderson and Peter Herriot (Eds.) *International handbook of selection and assessment*. Chichester: John Wiley & Sons.

Herriot, Peter and Pemberton, Carole (1995) *New deals: The revolution in managerial careers*. Chichester: John Wiley & Sons.

Herriot, Peter, Hirsh, Wendy and Reilly, Peter (1998) *Trust and transition: Managing today's employment relationship*. Chichester: John Wiley & Sons.

Highhouse, Scott, Zickar, Michael J., Thorsteinson, Todd J., Stierwalt, Sandra L. and Slaughter, Jerel E. (1999) Assessing company employment image: An example in the fast food industry. *Personnel Psychology*, **52**, No. 1, Spring, 151–172.

Hirsh, Wendy and Jackson, Charles (1996) Ticket to ride or no place to go? *People Management*, 27 June, 20–25.

Hirsh, Wendy and Reilly, Peter (1998) Skills planning. *People Management*, 9 July, 38–41.

Holbeche, Linda (1995) Peering into the future of careers. *People Management*, 31 May, 26–28.

Holbeche, Linda (1998) *High flyers and succession planning in changing organisations*. Roffey Park Management Institute.

Holton, Elwood F. and Russell, Craig J. (1997) The relationship of anticipation to newcomer socialization processes and outcomes: A pilot study. *Journal of Occupational and Organizational Psychology*, **70**, Part 2, 163–172.

Hope, Jeremy and Hope, Tony (1997) *Competing in the third wave*. Boston: Harvard Business School Press.

Houlder, Vanessa (1995) Misfortune of the lucky. *Financial Times*, 20 December.

Howard, Ann (1995) A framework for work change. Chapter 1 in Ann Howard (Ed.) *The changing nature of work*. San Francisco: Jossey-Bass Publishers.

Hunt, John W. (1998a) Generation X discovers that freedom is just another jail. *Financial Times*, 22 April.

Hunt, John W. (1998b) Questions of commitment. *Financial Times*, 20 May.

Hunt, John W. (1999a) Working in a rich human vein. *Financial Times*, 10 February.

Hunt, John W. (1999b) An outside advantage. *Financial Times*, 24 February.

Hunt, John W. and Laing, Bette (1997) Leadership: The role of the exemplar. *Business Strategy Review*, **8**, No. 1, 31–42.

Huselid, Mark A. (1994) Documenting HR's effect on company performance. *HR Magazine*, January, 79–85.

Huselid, Mark A. (1995) The impact of human resource management practices on turnover, productivity, and corporate financial performance. *Academy of Management Journal*, **38**, No. 3, 635–672.

Institute of Personnel and Development (1997) *The IPD guide on international management development*. London: The Institute of Personnel and Development.

Jackson, Paul R. (1997) Downsizing and deselection. Chapter 31 in Neil Anderson and Peter Herriot (Eds.) *International handbook of selection and assessment*. Chichester: John Wiley & Sons.

Jackson, Tony (1998a) When the big chair is vacant. *Financial Times*, 6 February.

Jackson, Tony (1998b) Growing pains from excess of success. *Financial Times*, 12 May.

Jackson, Tony (1998c) How to manage when your output is people. *Financial Times*, 14 May.

Jain, R. K. and Triandis, H. C. (1997) *Management of research and development organizations: Managing the unmanageable*. 2nd edition. New York: John Wiley & Sons.

Jansen, Paul G. W. (1997) Assessment in a technological world. Chapter 6 in Neil Anderson and Peter Herriot (Eds.) *International handbook of selection and assessment*. Chichester: John Wiley & Sons.

Jansen, Paul and de Jongh, Ferry (1998) *Assessment centres: Indispensable instruments for the appraisal of management talent*. Chichester: John Wiley & Sons.

Janz, Brian D., Colquitt, Jason A. and Noe, Raymond A. (1997) Knowledge worker team effectiveness: The role of autonomy, interdependence, team development, and contextual support variables. *Personnel Psychology*, **50**, No. 4, 877–904.

Jencks, Charles (1996) What is post-modernism? 4th edition. London: Academy Editions.

Judge, Timothy A., Thoresen, Carl J., Pucik, Vladimir and Welbourne, Theresa M. (1999) Managerial coping with organizational change: A dispositional perspective. *Journal of Applied Psychology*, **84**, No. 1, February, 107–122.

Kahn, William A. (1996) Secure base relationships at work. Chapter 6 in Douglas T. Hall and Associates. *The career is dead – Long live the career: A relational approach to careers*. San Francisco: Jossey-Bass Publishers.

Kakabadse, Andrew and Parker, Christopher (1984) Towards a theory of political behaviour in organizations. Chapter 5 in Andrew Kakabadse and Christopher Parker. *Power, politics, and organizations: A behavioural science view*. Chichester: John Wiley & Sons.

Kay, John (1998) We're all postmodern now. *Financial Times*, 28 April.

Kessler, Ian and Undy, Roger (1996) *The new employment relationship: Examining the psychological contract*. Issues in People Management No. 12. Institute of Personnel and Development.

Kidd, Jennifer M. (1997) Assessment for self-managed career development. Chapter 30 in Neil Anderson and Peter Herriot (Eds.) *International handbook of selection and assessment*. Chichester: John Wiley & Sons.

Kidd, Jennifer M. and Smewing, Chris (1997) Line manager support, career development, and organizational commitment. British Psychological Society

Occupational Psychology Conference, 7–9 January, *Book of Proceedings*. Leicester, England: British Psychological Society, pp. 101–106.

King, Zella and Guest, David (1998) A qualitative study of career self-management among graduate employees in early career. British Psychological Society Occupational Psychology Conference, 6–8 January, *Book of Proceedings*. Leicester, England: British Psychological Society, pp. 69–73.

Kinicki, A. J., Carson, K. P. and Bohlander, G. W. (1992) Relationship between an organization's actual human resource efforts and employee attitudes. *Group and Organization Management*, **17**, No. 2, 135–152.

Kinsman, Francis (1998) Proper selfishness for the greater benefit. *Royal Society of Arts Journal*, No. 1, 144.

Kirton, M. J. (1976) Adaptors and innovators: a description and measure. *Journal of Applied Psychology*, **61**, No. 5, 622–629.

Kirton, Michael (Ed.) (1994) *Adaptors and innovators: Styles of creativity and problem solving*. London: Routledge.

Kossek, Ellen E., Roberts, Karen, Fisher, Sandra and Demarr, Beverly (1998) Career self-management: A quasi-experimental assessment of the effects of a training intervention. *Personnel Psychology*, **51, No. 4, Winter, 935–962.**

Lado, Augustine A. and Wilson, Mary C. (1994) Human resource systems and sustained competitive advantage: A competency-based perspective. *Academy of Management Journal*, **19**, No. 4, 699–727.

Lancaster, Hal (1998) People are 'hot' again at work: A full staff is new management fad. *Wall Street Journal*, 5 May.

Latour, Almar and Coleman, Brian (1998) Volvo will lay off 6,000 in effort to reduce costs. *Wall Street Journal*, 1 December.

Lawler, Edward E. (1994) From job-based to competency-based organizations. *Journal of Organizational Behavior*, **15**, 3–15.

Leavitt, Harold J. and Whisler, Thomas L. (1958) Management in the 1980s. *Harvard Business Review*, November–December, 41–48.

Lewis, William and Harris, Clay (1998) US chief quits Deutsche Bank amid dispute over strategy. *Financial Times*, 28 February.

Lex Column (1998) Lasmo. *Financial Times*, 28 November.

Lipin, Steven (1998) Latest Lazard Freres aide to bid adieu: Rosenfeld, Investment banking chief. *Wall Street Journal*, 31 March.

Littlefield, David (1997) IT firms desperate to keep in-demand staff. *People Management*, 1 May 8.

McCall, Morgan W. (1998) *High Flyers: Developing the next generation of leaders*. Boston: Harvard Business School Press.

McCaul, Harriette S., Hinsz, Verlin B. and McCaul, Kevin D. (1995) Assessing organizational commitment: An employee's global attitude toward the organization. *Journal of Applied Behavioral Science*, **31**, No. 1, March, 80–90.

Macauley, Steve and Harding, Nigel (1996) Drawing up a new careers contract. *People Management*, 4 April, 34–35.

McGregor, D. (1960) *The human side of enterprise*. New York: McGraw-Hill.

McGuire, Patrick A. (1998) Wanted: Workers with flexibility for 21st century jobs. *American Psychological Association Monitor*, July, 10–12.

MacLachlan, Rob (1998a) Regeneration X. *People Management*, 2 April, 35–41.

MacLachlan, Rob (1998b) HR with attitude. *People Management*, 13 August, 36–39.

Maitland, Alison. (1998a) Reality bites for young recruits. *Financial Times*, 1 April.

Maitland, Alison (1998b) Women hand on their breakthrough tactics. *Financial Times*, 30 April.

Maitland, Alison (1998c) Forgotten but not gone: A remote risk. *Financial Times*, 5 May.

Markoff, John (1999) Privacy issues prompt change to Windows: Microsoft to remove identifying numbers. *International Herald Tribune*, 8 March.

Martinson, Jane (1998) Barings pair resign after row with ING. *Financial Times*, 11 April.

Mathieu, John E. and Zajac, Dennis M. (1990) A review and meta-analysis of the antecedents, correlates, and consequences of organizational commitment. *Psychological Bulletin*, **108**, No. 2, 171–194.

Maurer, Todd J. and Tarulli, Beverly A. (1994) Investigation of perceived environment, perceived outcome, and person variables in relationship to voluntary development activity by employees. *Journal of Applied Psychology*, **79**, No. 1, February, 3–14.

Mayo, Andrew (1991) *Managing careers: Strategies for organizations*. London: IPM.

Meyer, John P. and Allen, Natalie J. (1997) *Commitment in the workplace: Theory, research, and application*. Thousand Oaks, Calif.: Sage.

Michael, Christine (1998) The prime of Anthony Cross. *What Investment*, August, 10–11.

Mikulincer, Mario (1998) Attachment working models and the sense of trust: An exploration of interaction goals and affect regulation. *Journal of Personality and Social Psychology*, **74**, No. 5, 1209–1224.

Miles, Raymond E. and Snow, Charles C. (1978) *Organizational strategy, structure, and process*. New York: McGraw-Hill.

Miles, Raymond E. and Snow, Charles C. (1996) Twenty-first-century careers. Chapter 6 in Michael B. Arthur and Denise M. Rousseau (Eds.) *The boundaryless career*. New York: Oxford University Press.

Mirvis, Philip H. and Hall, Douglas T. (1996a) Psychological success and the boundaryless career. Chapter 14 in Michael B. Arthur and Denise M. Rousseau (Eds.) *The boundaryless career*. New York: Oxford University Press.

Mirvis, Philip H. and Hall, Douglas T. (1996b) New organizational forms and the new career. Chapter 3 in Douglas T. Hall and Associates. *The career is dead – Long live the career: A relational approach to careers*. San Francisco: Jossey-Bass Publishers.

Mohrman, Susan Albers and Cohen, Susan G. (1995) When people get out of the box: New relationships, new systems. Chapter 10 in Ann Howard (Ed.) *The changing nature of work*. San Francisco: Jossey-Bass Publishers.

Murray, Bridget (1998) Notion of a life long career is now a thing of the past. *American Psychological Association Monitor*, May, 35.

O'Brien, Timothy L. and Truell, Peter (1998) At Citigroup, fears of exodus. *International Herald Tribune*, 4 November.

O'Neill, Brian (1997) Predicting managers' performance from their traits, values and thinking styles. Paper presented to British Psychological Society Annual Conference, Edinburgh.

Parkes, Christopher (1998) Boeing's shares fall 17% after profits warning. *Financial Times*, 3 December.

Patterson, Malcolm G., West, Michael A., Lawthom, Rebecca and Nickell, Stephen (1997) *Impact of people management practices on business performance*. Issues in People Management No. 22. London: Institute of Personnel and Development.

Pfeffer, Jeffrey (1994) *Competitive advantage through people: Unleashing the power of the work force*. Boston, Mass.: Harvard Business School Press.

Pfeffer, Jeffrey (1998) *The human equation: Building profits by putting people first*. Boston, Mass.: Harvard Business School Press.

Pickard, Jane (1997a) Vacational qualifications. *People Management*, 10 July, 26–31.

Pickard, Jane (1997b) Talent-spotting NatWest tackles inverted ageism. *People Management*, 23 October, 31.

Pickard, Jane (1997c) Future organisations will need higher IQs. *People Management*, 4 December, 15.

Pitfield, Michael (1998) Here endeth the lesson. *People Management*, 19 February, 29.

Prickett, Ruth (1998a) Stateside statistics show significance of soft skills. *People Management*, 5 March, 19.

Prickett, Ruth (1998b) Employers warned against overselling graduate jobs. *People Management*, 16 April, 20.

Prickett, Ruth (1998c) Staff value a career path above salary. *People Management*, 16 April, 17.

Prickett, Ruth (1998d) Firms complain of quality shortfall among students. *People Management*, 9 July, 10.

Pritchard, Stephen (1996) Branch manager? Don't bank on it. *The Independent*, 11 April.

Pucik, Vladimir (1998) Creating leaders that are world class. Mastering Global Business Supplement. *Financial Times*.

Quinn, R. E. and Rohrbaugh, J. (1981) A competing values approach to organizational effectiveness. *Public Productivity Review*, **5**, 122–140.

Rajan, Amin and van Eupen, Penny (1997) Take it from the top. *People Management*, 23 October, 26–34.

Refaussé, John (1996) Self-knowledge to lift career spirits. *People Management*, 16 May, 34–35.

Reichheld, Frederick F. (1996) *The loyalty effect: The hidden force behind growth, profits, and lasting value*. Boston, Mass.: Harvard Business School Press.

Robinson, David F. and Miner, Anne S. (1996) Careers change as organizations learn. Chapter 5 in Michael B. Arthur and Denise M. Rousseau (Eds.) *The boundaryless career*. New York: Oxford University Press.

Rousseau, Denise M. (1990) New-hire perceptions of their own and their employer's obligations: A study of psychological contracts. *Journal of Organizational Behavior*, **11**, 389–400.

Rousseau, Denise M. and Wade-Benzoni, Kimberly A. (1995) Changing individual–organization attachments. Chapter 8 in Ann Howard (Ed.) *The changing nature of work*. San Francisco: Jossey-Bass Publishers.

Ruddle, Keith, Stewart, Rosemary and Dopson, Sue (1998) From downsizing to revitalisation. Mastering Global Business Supplement. *Financial Times*.

Saxenian, Annalee (1996) Beyond boundaries: Open labor markets and learning in Silicon Valley. Chapter 2 in Michael B. Arthur and Denise M. Rousseau (Eds.) *The boundaryless career*. New York: Oxford University Press.

Schaubroeck, John, Ganster, Daniel C. and Jones, James R. (1998) Organization and occupation influences in the attraction–selection–attrition process. *Journal of Applied Psychology*, **83**, No. 6, 869–891.

Schein, Edgar H. (1978) *Career dynamics: Matching individual and organizational needs*. Reading, Mass.: Addison-Wesley.

Schein, Edgar H. (1997) Organizational learning: What is new? MIT Sloan School of Management. http://www.learning.mit.edu/res/wp/10012.html.

Schneider, Benjamin (1987) The people make the place. *Personnel Psychology*, **40**, 437–453.

Schneider, Benjamin, Smith, D. Brent, Taylor, Sylvester and Fleenor, John (1998) Personality and organizations: A test of the homogeneity of personality hypothesis. *Journal of Applied Psychology*, **83**, No. 3, 462–470.

Schofield, Philip (1998) Give the transferable skill your vote if you want to get selected. *Daily Telegraph*, 2 April.

Schweiger, D. M. and DeNisi, A. S. (1991) Communication with employees following a merger: A longitudinal field experiment. *Academy of Management Journal*, **34**, 110–135.

Seegers, Jeroen J. J. L. (1997) Assessing development needs. Chapter 29 in Neil Anderson and Peter Herriot (Eds.) *International handbook of selection and assessment*. Chichester: John Wiley & Sons.

Sennett, Richard (1998) Work can screw you up. *Financial Times*, 17 October.

Shackleton, Viv and Newell, Sue (1997) International assessment and selection. Chapter 4 in Neil Anderson and Peter Herriot (Eds.) *International handbook of selection and assessment*. Chichester: John Wiley & Sons.

Shaffer, Margaret A. and Harrison, David A. (1998) Expatriates' psychological withdrawal from international assignments: Work, nonwork, and family influences. *Personnel Psychology*, **51**, No. 1, Spring, 87–118.

Sims, Ronald R. (1994) Human resource management's role in clarifying the new psychological contract. *Human Resource Management*, **33**, No. 3, 373–382.

Sleek, Scott (1998) Some corporate mergers, like marriages, end up on the rocks. *American Psychological Association Monitor*, July, 13.

Snow, Charles C. and Snell, Scott A. (1993) Staffing as strategy. Chapter 4 in Neal Schmitt, Walter C. Borman and Associates (Eds.) *Personnel selection in organizations*. San Francisco: Jossey-Bass Publishers.

Sonnenfeld, Jeffrey A. and Peiperl, Maury A. (1988) Staffing policy as a strategic response: A typology of career systems. *Academy of Management Review*, **13**, No. 4, 588–600.

Sorrentino, Richard M., Holmes, John G., Hanna, Steven E. and Sharp, Ann (1995) Uncertainty orientation and trust in close relationships: Individual differences in cognitive styles. *Journal of Personality and Social Psychology*, **68**, No. 2, 314–327.

Sparrow, Paul R. and Bognanno, Mario (1993) Competency requirement forecasting: Issues for international selection and assessment. *International Journal of Selection and Assessment*, **1**, No. 1, January, 50–58.

Sternberg, Robert J. (1997) Tacit knowledge and job success. Chapter 10 in Neil Anderson and Peter Herriot (Eds.) *International handbook of selection and assessment*. Chichester: John Wiley & Sons.

Stewart, Thomas A. (1997) *Intellectual capital: The new wealth of organisations*. London: Nicholas Brealey Publishing.

Storey, John, Edwards, Paul and Sisson, Keith (1997) *Managers in the making: Careers, development and control in corporate Britain and Japan*. Thousand Oaks, Calif.: Sage.

Sturges, Jane (1998) What it means to succeeed: Personal conceptions of career success held by male and female managers at different ages. British Psychological Society Occupational Psychology Conference, 6–8 January, *Book of Proceedings*. Leicester, England: British Psychological Society, pp. 15–19.

Summers, Diane (1998) Generation X comes of age. *Financial Times*, 16 February.

Taylor, Russell (1997) Taking stock. *Money Management*, November, 28.

Timmins, Nicholas (1998) Looking abroad for IT skills. *Financial Times*, 27 February.

Toffler, Alvin (1980) *The third wave*. London: Pan Books.

Urry, Maggie (1999) A lack of executive flair signals trouble at the top. *Financial Times*, 3 March.

Van der Spiegel, Jan (1995) New information technologies and changes in work. In Ann Howard (Ed.) *The changing nature of work*. San Francisco: Jossey-Bass Publishers.

Van Maanen, John and Schein, Edgar H (1979) Toward a theory of organizational socialization. In Barry M. Staw (Ed.) *Research in organizational behavior*. **1**, pp. 209–264, Greenwich, Conn.: JAI Press, Inc.

Wagstyl, Stefan and Bowley, Graham (1998) A strategist who has everything to play for. *Financial Times*, 20 April.

Walsh, Jennie (1998) Comeuppance for the CEO who devalued his people. *People Management*, 9 July, 14.

Waters, Richard (1998a) Without a care in the world. *Financial Times*, 7 March.

Waters, Richard (1998b) The squeeze in on. *Financial Times*, 4 May.

Webber, Alan M. (1993) What's so new about the new economy? *Harvard Business Review*, **25**, January–February, 24–42.

Weick, Karl E. (1996) Enactment and the boundaryless career: Organizing as we work. Chapter 3 in Michael B. Arthur and Denise M. Rousseau (Eds.) *The boundaryless career*. New York: Oxford University Press.

Welch, Jilly (1997) Students swap status for pay and potential. *People Management*, 24 July, 17.

Welch, Jilly (1998a) Polygram offers £24m to stem exodus of key staff. *People Management*, 9 July, 9.

Welch, Jilly (1998b) Lloyds/TSB give staff 'job for life'. *People Management*, 1 October, 12.

Welch, Jilly (1999) Firms struggle to fill posts despite graduate surplus. *People Management*, 14 January, 13.

White, Gregory L. (1998) Daimler-Benz ads bypass consumers. *Wall Street Journal*, 16 November.

Whitehead, Mark (1998) 'Recruit in haste, repent at leisure', survey warns. *People Management*, 9 July, 13.

Williams, Allan P. O. and Dobson, Paul (1997) Personnel selection and corporate strategy. Chapter 11 in Neil Anderson and Peter Herriot (Eds.) *International handbook of selection and assessment*. Chichester: John Wiley & Sons.

Wills, Jackie (1997) Can do better. *Personnel Today*, 5 June, 31–34.

Winsborough, David, Blagdon, Jenny, Brown, Sarah and Aitken, Paul (1997) Sense and sensibility: A new career management at Mobil Oil New Zealand. British Psychological Society Occupational Psychology Conference, 7–9 January, *Book of Proceedings*. Leicester, England: British Psychological Society, pp. 149–154.

Woodruffe, Charles (1993) *Assessment centres: Identifying and developing competence*, 2nd edition. London: IPD.

Woodruffe, Charles (1997) Going back a generation. *People Management*, 20 February, 32–34.

Woodruffe, Charles and Wylie, Robert (1994) Going the whole hog: The design of development centres at NatWest. *Competency*, **2**, No. 1, Autumn, 23–27.

Wooldridge, Ewart (1998) Thoughts from the chair. *Career Path: A quarterly IPD newsletter for forum members*, **23**, Spring, 1.

Worrall, Les and Cooper, Cary L. (1997) *The quality of working life: 1997 survey of managers' changing experiences*. London: Institute of Management.

Worrall, Les and Cooper, Cary L. (1998) *The quality of working life: 1998 survey of managers' changing experiences*. London: Institute of Management.

Yeung, Rob and McBride, John (1998) Job losses – how to treat the survivors. *Financial Times*, 23 September.

Yukl, G. and van Fleet, D. D. (1992) Theory and research on leadership in organizations. In M. D. Dunnette and L. M. Hough (Eds.) *Handbook of industrial and organizational psychology*, **3**, 2nd edition, pp. 147–197. Palo Alto, Calif.: Consulting Psychologists Press.

# Index of First Named Authors

# Subject index